Th

FUTURE VOLUMES
WILL INCLUDE

The Essential Wyatt

❖❖

Sir Thomas Wyatt

BORN 1503?
DIED 11 OCTOBER 1542

The Essential
WYATT

Selected and with an
Introduction by

W. S. MERWIN

The Ecco Press
New York

Introduction and selection copyright © 1989 by W. S. Merwin
All rights reserved
Published in 1989 by The Ecco Press
26 West 17th Street, New York, N.Y. 10011
Published simultaneously in Canada by
Penguin Books Canada Ltd., Ontario
Printed in the United States of America
Designed by Reg Perry

FIRST EDITION

Library of Congress Cataloging-in-Publication Data
Wyatt, Thomas, Sir, 1503?–1542.
The essential Wyatt.
(The Essential poets; v. 10)
I. Merwin, W. S. (William Stanley), 1927–
II. Title. III. Series.
PR2401.M47   1988   821'.2   88-28356

ISBN 0-88001-180-7

Portrait of Sir Thomas Wyatt
by Hans Holbein,
from the Royal Collection.
Windsor Castle, Royal Library.
Copyright © Her Majesty Queen Elizabeth II.

To Matthew and John

Contents

❖❖

The Essential Wyatt

❖❖

Introduction

❖❖

What we hear when we read the poems of Sir Thomas Wyatt, some four and a half centuries after he wrote them, is a fair example of the ways of that elusive but inescapable figure who haunts the imagination of the Renaissance: Fortuna, "that torneth as a ball." There is no way of knowing now what Wyatt's poems sounded like to his contemporaries. His lyrics for the lute must have circulated as songs, and his other poems were read in manuscript, but their reception, their readers, their fate are, with very few exceptions, unknown to us. We do not really know, either, where Wyatt acquired his sense of what was available and desirable in poetry in his time. Nor do we know with whom he might have discussed such matters and talked over his free translations from the Italian, and his sonnets, which are said to be the first written in English. We know of a few of his contemporaries with whom he shared interests in such things. The Earl of Surrey, for one. But Wyatt and Surrey were separated by station and by political and religious differences as well as age (Wyatt was Surrey's elder by fourteen years). Nevertheless, Surrey wrote three poems in praise of Wyatt's gifts and character, and it is worth noting that the first of them, a sonnet in honor of Wyatt's "Translations of the Psalms"—clearly Wyatt's "Penitential Psalms"—was composed with a prosodic freedom more characteristic of Wyatt's poems than of Surrey's. For most of Surrey's poems—in such marked contrast to Wyatt's that the comparison became an academic cliché—are remarkably regular, and their "smoothness" has found its advocates in every age. It seems to be the main quality that led a line of editors and critics from Tottel's day to the twentieth century to consider Surrey the more gifted of the two poets. The fact that the poems of Wyatt and Surrey both were first published

| 3 |

in *Tottel's Miscellany* in 1557 invited the comparison to begin with, even though Tottel had gone to the trouble of tampering extensively with Wyatt's lines to get them to scan to his satisfaction.

His metrical meddling emphasizes our ignorance of how Wyatt's readers in his own age received his poems. By the time *Tottel's Miscellany* was published, Wyatt had been dead for fifteen years. During that time the literate fashion had been moving in favor of metrical regularity. No doubt there is always a taste for it, more pronounced and encouraged in some ages and circles, and in some readers, than in others, and perhaps there are always exceptions, too. The poets of Wyatt's generation had been just that much closer not only to Chaucer but also to the relatively free prosody of Middle English poetry, and to the archaic versions of the ballads; it is hard for us to imagine how those influenced the way they heard and conceived of iambic pentameter, and the way they wrote altogether. Obviously some of their writing suffers from lack of talent, of care, of skill, of sophistication, but it seems sweeping to suppose—as some editors have done—that all their departures from the imported iambic meter were the result of pure ineptitude, and that Wyatt's own metrical variations were nothing but his clumsy failures to conform to a regular pattern. If it seemed that way to the editor of *Tottel's Miscellany,* the opinion could not have been unanimous or it is unlikely that Wyatt's poems would have acquired the reputation that led to their publication and indeed to their occupying more of the *Miscellany* than the poems of anyone else including Surrey. It is hard to imagine that all of Wyatt's metrical roughnesses could have struck every reader at the time as entirely successful, but the beauty of many of them must have been evident to some readers from the beginning. And the taste for such prosodic syncopations clearly did not die out completely with Wyatt's generation. Others have commented on the affinity between the metrical complexities of Wyatt's poems and the still more pronounced prosodic inversions deliberately wrought, half a century later, by John Donne.

But the prevailing fashion, the conventions, the tradition of poetry in English, swept in a different direction as though it were the only one, and both Wyatt and Donne were all but ignored for most of three centuries. It was not until there were readers who could grasp and love the originality (in the sense of its relation to its source) and achievement of Hopkins that something at least of the power and beauty of Donne's poems and of Wyatt's could be rediscovered and heard again. Until then, Wyatt's reputation suffered from the opinions of editors and critics who could not hear as poetry any verse that departed from regular scansion, and for whom all such variations were the consequences—as Hyder Edward Rollins put it, in writing on *Tottel's Miscellany* in 1929—of the fact that Wyatt "was the pioneer who fumbled in the linguistic difficulties that beset him and prepared the way for Surrey's smoother lines and more pleasing accentuation." It was E. K. Chambers, focusing his attention upon Wyatt himself in the twenties and early thirties of this century (*Sir Thomas Wyatt and Some Collected Studies* was published in 1933), who rescued Wyatt at once from the improvements of previous editors and the metrical prissiness of former critics, and in so doing made some clear and important—and, it now seems, rather obvious—distinctions.

There are the poems that were written either to be sung or as though they were intended to be sung. The notion that Wyatt was a metrical clod might have been shaken by an examination—and above all by a reading aloud—of these poems. "The range of metrical variation," Chambers noted, "is very wide; more than seventy distinct stanza forms are to be found in the hundred and twenty examples. The basis is nearly always iambic." The forms, as he says, "are those known in the neo-Latin poetry of the *vagantes* and analysed in medieval treatises on poetics. Many of them also appear in earlier vernacular poetry. Here Wyatt is at the end rather than the beginning of a tradition. He handles it as a master, with a facility of rhythmical accomplishment to which his Elizabethan successors, although they had many qualities which he had not, rarely attained."

In speaking of the other poems, particularly the love poems, Chambers compares Wyatt with Petrarch, whom Wyatt translated. Wyatt, Chambers says, unlike Petrarch, "does not dwell upon the physical beauty of his lady. . . . He does not couple her in proud compare of everything that is in heaven and earth; there is but one perfunctory allusion to lilies and roses. Nor of course does he, like Petrarch, veil her in that circumambient penumbra of spirituality. He makes little use of visual imagery. His range of metaphor is restricted and rather conventional. For the most part he is content with the plainest of words, and relies for his effect upon his rhythmical accomplishment. This economy of speech gives him at times a singular plangency. In appeal or reproach every line tells like a hammer-stroke. . . .

"Nor does Wyatt," Chambers continues, "at all foreshadow the Elizabethans, with their lavishness, their passion for visible things, their ready flow of coloured utterance." It is in this comparison that Chambers suggests that "Wyatt's real affinities, if with any, are with John Donne. He has not Donne's depth of fiery and often turbid thought. His is a soul of lighter make. But there is something of the same characteristic poise."

Chambers, of course, intended no detraction from Wyatt in comparing him to Donne. He was suggesting a sympathy. But as we have seen, Wyatt's posthumous reputation has been afflicted repeatedly by comparisons, many of which were quite unjust; he has been blamed for not having another's talent and writing like someone else, and I have no wish to continue the practice, in suggesting yet another comparison from outside the course of English poetry altogether. For years Wyatt has seemed to me one of the very few figures in the language whose writing bore some relation, however distant and slight, to the great poems of François Villon. The differences are immediately obvious—differences of scale, of range, of volume and audacity, and of tragic power. As Chambers notes in comparing Wyatt with Donne, Wyatt does not have Villon's "depth of fiery and often turbid thought" either, and his "soul [is] of lighter make," I suppose. But I have not suggested the kinship in order to minimize Wyatt. The affinity with Villon, I think, is there in some of Wyatt's great songs, in which like Villon he uses—and masterfully—the exquisite delicacy of the late medieval lyric to articulate a harshness and irony of subject and feeling that can be startlingly at odds with the form, and the result is the creation of a peculiar tension and power. Wyatt accomplishes it with his characteristic lightness of touch, usually. But not always, and the passages closest to Villon are those in which the lyric conveys irony, frustration, and in a few places rage:

> Perchaunce the lye wethered and old,
> The wynter nyghtes that are so cold,
>   Playnyng in vain vnto the mone;
> Thy wisshes then dare not be told;
>   Care then who lyst, for I have done.

> And then may chaunce the to repent
> The tyme that thou hast lost and spent
>   To cause thy lovers sigh and swoune;
> Then shalt thou knowe beaultie but lent,
>   And wisshe and want as I have done.

It was writing like this, which includes of course some of his best-known poems, that first attracted me to Wyatt when I was a student, and it was the cranky artistry not just of his prosody but of his language as a whole, its mixture of bluntness and grace, directness and song, that first drew me to his poetry. Among the poems in this vein is the famous sonnet "Who so list to hount, I knowe where is an hynde"—number 7 in *The Egerton Ms.* I mention it not only because of its extraordinary beauty and life but also as an example of Wyatt's real originality.

The poem has been taken to refer, along with several others, to Wyatt's love affair with Anne Boleyn before Henry VIII laid claim to her. There is no way of knowing with certainty whether Wyatt and Anne Boleyn were ever actually lovers, and the sonnet itself is a translation from Petrarch. But whether the writing in English alludes to Anne Boleyn or not, it comes to us with the mysterious force of an intensely personal poem. The enigmatic nature of it is compounded by the fact that the line that seems most germane to the Anne Boleyn legend, *"Noli me tangere,* for Caesars I ame," is already there, at least in part, in the Italian. But the imperative phrase there is in Italian, not in Wyatt's dramatic Latin. *"Nessun mi tocchi"* are Petrarch's words, and the writing on the doe's collar, in his poem, says that "my Caesar's will is to make me free." Wyatt turns that to something far more intimate, tense, and conflicting: his "for Caesars I ame / And wylde for to hold, though I seme tame." The possession has been turned round, it may be noted. It is no longer "my Caesar," but "Caesars I ame." And incidentally, it would be hard to find a line in Wyatt that is a better example of his mastery of metrical variation and roughness for charging a line with dramatic intensity.

A close comparison of Wyatt's poem with the Petrarch original reveals this kind of dramatic shift again and again. The Italian sonnet seems to be a relatively conventional medieval dream poem: a vision of an enticing and haughty *white* doe *appears* to the speaker, who abandons all his labors to follow her, as the miser pursues the allurement of wealth. Wyatt turns this around too, and it is the "vayne travaille" of the pursuit itself that has wearied him until he has fallen back and given up the chase. "I leve of therefore, / Sins in a nett I seke to hold the wynde." The image, like much else in the English, is wholly Wyatt's, as are the tone, the pace, the whole presence of the sonnet, including its warning, in the voice of experience: "Who list her hount, I put him owte of dowbte, / As well as I may spend his tyme in vain." Whatever their root in his life and his reading, the lines are clearly his own, and close to the central theme and imagery of his poetry. And while he may have been less concerned with describing the object of his passion than was Petrarch, this poem is laden with a heat and sensuality and a convincing erotic bitterness nowhere to be found in the Italian sonnet on which it was based. Wyatt's poem, I think, is an exception to Kenneth Muir's assertion that Wyatt's sonnets were not among his best poems. In this sonnet the force and beauty, the authority and originality are evident whether or not we think of the poem as a translation, and whether or not we know to whom it refers or indeed whether it refers to any single affair or person. The feelings that made it and give it its urgency and authenticity obviously had their source in something real in Wyatt's life, but we are unlikely to find out more about them anywhere except in the poems.

Wyatt's biography, in fact, is one more of those Tudor and Elizabethan *vitae* that tell us tantalizingly little of which we can be sure, but we know more about Wyatt than we do of many other poets of the age, including perhaps Shakespeare. And we do have a portrait painted by Holbein. Wyatt was born in 1503 at Allington Castle on the river Medway. The castle had not been a family estate for very long, but had been given to Wyatt's father, Sir Henry, as a recompense for services and sufferings on behalf of the house of Tudor. Wyatt was present at court when he was still a child. He attended the christening of Princess Mary when he was twelve or thirteen, and he went to St. John's College, Cambridge, soon afterward. He married in 1520, when he was seventeen. His wife was Lord Cobham's daughter Elizabeth. They had two children, Thomas and Bess, but Elizabeth was unfaithful to him, and they separated.

Wyatt embarked on a diplomatic career when he was twenty-two, accompanying the English ambassador to France in 1525, returning to England with official dispatches, then accompanying Sir John Russell, the English emissary to the pope, in 1526. In Italy he was captured by the Spanish, and managed to escape while his release was being negotiated. Other missions followed in the next few years and he took his father's place as chief ewer at the coronation of Anne Boleyn.

Their relation has been the subject of more romantic speculation than anything else in his life. There is circumstantial evidence to suggest that Wyatt's life and fate were for a while associated with hers, and there are several contemporary stories that are quite specific about what the relationship was, and what became of it. A contemporary of Wyatt's named Nicholas Sanders declared Anne and Wyatt had been lovers and that when Wyatt learned Henry VIII planned to marry her he told the Privy Council she was not a fit wife for the king. According to the story, Henry refused to believe what he was told and banished Wyatt from the court. Other writers told variants of the story, but it has been noted that they were biased—as Catholics these critics were happy to find or invent scurrilous or damaging stories about Anne at the time of her trial. Kenneth Muir (whose lucid summary of the probabilities forms part of his introduction to the Muses' Library edition of Wyatt, which I have used for this selection) is inclined to believe that there had been an affair, no doubt a rather dark and vexed one, between Wyatt and Anne Boleyn, and that the lines

> *sins I did refrayne*
> *Her that did set our country in a rore*

refer to Anne. Wyatt, for whatever reasons, was imprisoned and then banished to his castle in 1536, shortly before Anne's exposure, but was released in the summer of that year and given new official posts. He was appointed ambassador to Spain in the following year.

But his troubles were far from over. Besides his affairs of the heart, whatever they may have been, Wyatt had enemies at court, and we do not know how many of his tribulations they contrived. His finances, by now, were "chaotic," in Kenneth Muir's word, and were rescued from that state by the good offices of a friend and patron, Cromwell. In his late thirties Wyatt suffered the death of his father and the execution of this same friend Cromwell. Several of Wyatt's most personal poems—a few of them, again, evolved from translations—

allude to this second appalling loss. The execution of Cromwell in the summer of 1540 was one event in a chain of intrigues that threatened Wyatt as well. At the beginning of the following year he was arrested and all his possessions seized. He was accused by the bishop of London of a list of offenses that included treason and immorality.

Wyatt defended himself vigorously and cogently, not only parrying the charges against him but also taking the initiative and attacking his accuser.

"I know no man that did you dishonour," ran his reply to the bishop, "but your unmannerly behaviour, that made ye a laughing stock to all men that came in your company, and me sometime sweat for shame to see you." And he pressed the charge of immorality too upon its author. "Come on now, my Lord of London, what is my abominable and vicious living? Do ye know it, or have ye heard it? I grant I do not profess chastity; but yet I use not abomination. If ye know it, tell it here, with whom and when. If ye heard it, who is your author? Have ye seen me have any harlot in my house whilst ye were in my company? Did you ever see woman so much as dine, or sup, at my table? None, but for your pleasure, the woman that was in the galley; which I assure you may well be seen; for, before you came, neither she nor any other came above the mast. But because the gentlemen took pleasure to see you entertain her, therefore they made her dine and sup with you; and they liked well your looks, your carving to Madonna, your drinking to her, and your playing under the table. Ask Mason, ask Blage—Bowes is dead—ask Wolf, that was my steward; they can tell how the gentlemen marked it, and talked of it. It was a play to them, the keeping of your bottles, that no man might drink of but yourself; and 'that the little fat priest were a jolly morsel for the Signora.' This was their talk; it is not my devise: ask other, whether I do lie."

Wyatt was cleared of the accusations against him, and released with a full pardon. He was given further diplomatic missions, was elected to

Parliament, was made a vice admiral of the fleet. In 1542, when he was thirty-nine, he set out for Falmouth, to meet a Spanish emissary to the court. He was stricken with a fever on the way there, died at Sherborne, and is buried there.

What we know of his character comes partly from such bare facts, partly from the testimony of a few of those who knew him, and for the rest, from his poems. The milieu in which he lived gave rise to intense loyalties and ruthless defamation, and he had his share of both. In those poems where his voice is clearest, we hear someone who is forthright, independent, sensual, and dignified. He was under few illusions concerning the life at court and its deceptions, and some of his sharpest and most vigorous writing arises from his sense of the falsity of many of the assumptions and circumstances that claimed the greater part of his life.

> Stond who so list upon the Slipper toppe
>   Of courtes estates, and lett me heare reioyce;
> And vse me quyet without lett or stoppe,
>   Vnknowen in courte, that hath suche brackishe ioyes:
>   In hidden place, so lett my dayes forthe passe,
>   That when my yeares be done, withouten noyse,
>   I may dye aged after the common trace.
> For hym death greep'the right hard by the croppe
>   That is moche knowen of other; and of him self alas,
>   Doth dye vnknowen, dazed with dreadfull face.

The poem, according to Kenneth Muir, is one of those written after the execution of Cromwell, and it is full of intimate and bitter urgency. Yet it is also true that it, too, like the love poems, has its place in a broad and ancient tradition—a convention, indeed—of decrying worldly life and asserting a preference for rustic simplicity and seclusion. There is no reason to suppose, because of this alone, or because Wyatt did not spend the remainder of his life in rural seclusion and voluntary poverty, that the impulse and feelings behind his poems in this vein are not genuine, any more than we should dismiss the love poems as mere conventions simply because a convention lends them form and style.

Indeed, the play of contraries in Wyatt—convention and directness, craving and withdrawal—makes him more interesting, personal, intimate than his contemporaries. He has been criticized for the narrowness of his range, and it is true that the basic attitudes he articulates, the underlying dramatic positions and images, are relatively few. His was not, we should remember, a life wholly dedicated to poetry, as were Chaucer's or Shakespeare's, Milton's or Wordsworth's. He was an aristocratic amateur and poetry, for him, was perforce an avocation—one to which he was clearly born, nevertheless, and which he must have practiced on occasion, to judge from the poems alone, with a compelling passion. One of the central attitudes (in the theatrical sense) in his poetry is the lover's reproach to the unfeeling beloved, either for ignoring his passion or for betraying it at some later time. The theme is one of the most familiar of all the conventions of European poetry from the age of chivalry to the seventeenth century. But in Wyatt's best poems it takes on a singular complexity of immediate and conflicting feeling. Such poems as "They fle from me" or "My lute awake!" or "Who so list to hount" vibrate with mixed feelings—desire, anger, mortification, mockery, bitterness, even tenderness. And some of the same complexity of feeling is present when the beloved is the worldly life itself of fortune and favor and fickle or loyal friends, and the poet speaks of his enforced or voluntary distance from it, scorning it, rejecting it, and at certain turns still fascinated and attracted by it. The tension serves to increase the intimacy and force of the language, and to fill it with that complex continuo, a haunting, dissonant, disabused yet sensual song that is Wyatt's alone. Once truly heard it is unlikely to be forgotten.

Or so it seems, speaking only from my own experience. The wry beauty of Wyatt's poems hung in my ear when I was a student, and then and since exercised some indefinable influence upon what I heard and relished and listened for in other poetry. He has been indifferently served by anthologists, even in modern times. A number of his finest poems appear again and again, but others remarkable for the beauty and life of their language have never been anthologized at all, and some of them, such as "Stond who so list" or "Ye old mule," reveal facets of Wyatt's talent and sensibility that are generally overlooked, so that the range of his gift seems more limited than it really is.

But he is—as many poets seem, after four centuries—an uneven poet, and I have indulged my fondness for him by including here and there poems which, while they certainly do not strike me as wholly successful, contain passages which have given me pleasure for so long that I have been reluctant to pass up a chance to call attention to them. "Passe forth, my wonted cryes" is simply one more lyric in a much wonted vein until one comes to the strength and freshness of

> *For though hard rockes among*
>   *She semes to haue bene bred,*
> *And of the Tigre long*
>   *Bene nourished and fed:*
> *Yet shall that nature change,*
>   *If pitie once win place,*
> *Whom as vnknowen and strange*
>   *She now away doth chase*
>
> *And as the water soft,*
>   *Without forcyng or strength,*
> *Where that it falleth oft,*
>   *Hard stones doth perse at length:*
> *So in her stony hart*
>   *My plaintes at last shall graue,*
> *And, rygour set apart,*
>   *Winne grant of that I craue.*

But choosing from among the "Penitential Psalms" presented particular difficulties, quite apart from a lack of enthusiasm for the material. They were written all at once, in 1540, when Wyatt had retired to his castle at Allington after the execution of Cromwell, and when no doubt he fully expected the further misfortunes soon to descend upon him. The psalms were composed with prologues that linked them into a single poem relating the story of David and Bathsheba as a setting for the psalms themselves and their penitence. The text as we have it is Wyatt's first draft, which apparently he never had a chance to revise, and it is useless to speculate about what he might have done. There are fine passages—most of them brief—throughout, but the prologues, in their ponderous stanzas, exercise a freedom of movement rare in the psalms, whose beauty, except for individual lines and phrases, is in the weighty nobility of the language.

As mentioned previously, I have based my selections of the poems, and the historical sections of these notes, on Kenneth Muir's Muses' Library edition, *Sir Thomas Wyatt: The Collected Poems* (Routledge & Kegan Paul, 1949) which has been my companion since soon after it was published. Of the principal critical works on Wyatt, the most important doubtless is E. K. Chambers's *Sir Thomas Wyatt and Some Collected Studies.* Kenneth Muir's introduction acknowledges his debt to Chambers, which is shared by everyone who has come to love the poems of Wyatt during the past fifty years.

—W. S. MERWIN

Poems

❖

♦ ♦ ♦ ♦ ♦

Behold, love, thy power how she dispiseth!
My great payne how litle she regardeth!
　The holy oth, wherof she taketh no cure,
　Broken she hath; and yet she bideth sure
Right at her ease and litle she dredeth.
Wepened thou art, and she vnarmed sitteth;
To the disdaynfull her liff she ledeth,
　To me spitefull withoute cause or mesure,
　　Behold, love.

I ame in hold: if pitie the meveth,
Goo bend thy bowe, that stony hertes breketh,
　And with some stroke revenge the displeasure
　Of the and him, that sorrowe doeth endure,
And, as his lorde, the lowly entreateth.
　　Behold, love.

♦ ♦ ♦ ♦ ♦

Caesar, when that the traytor of Egipt
　With th'onourable hed did him present,
　Covering his gladnes, did represent
　Playnt with his teres owteward, as it is writt:
And Hannyball eke, when fortune him shitt

Clene from his reign and from all his intent,
Laught to his folke, whome sorrowe did torment,
His cruell dispite for to disgorge and qwit.
So chaunceth it oft that every passion
The mynde hideth, by colour contrary,
With fayned visage, now sad, now mery.
Whereby if I laught, any tyme or season
It is for bicause I have nother way
To cloke my care, but vnder sport and play.

♦ ♦ ♦ ♦ ♦

The longe love, that in my thought doeth harbar
And in myn hert doeth kepe his residence,
Into my face preseth with bolde pretence,
And therin campeth, spreding his baner.
She that me lerneth to love and suffre,
And willes that my trust and lustes negligence
Be rayned by reason, shame and reverence,
With his hardines taketh displeasur.
Wherewithall, vnto the hertes forrest he fleith,
Leving his entreprise with payn and cry;
And ther him hideth, and not appereth.
What may I do when my maister fereth
But in the feld with him to lyve and dye?
For goode is the liff, ending faithfully.

♦ ♦ ♦ ♦ ♦

Who so list to hount, I knowe where is an hynde,
But as for me, helas, I may no more:
The vayne travaill hath weried me so sore.

I ame of theim that farthest commeth behinde;
Yet may I by no meanes my weried mynde
   Drawe from the Diere: but as she fleeth afore,
Faynting I folowe. I leve of therefore,
   Sins in a nett I seke to hold the wynde.
Who list her hount, I put him owte of dowbte,
   As well as I may spend his tyme in vain:
   And, graven with Diamonds, in letters plain
There is written her faier neck rounde abowte:
   Noli me tangere, for Caesars I ame;
   And wylde for to hold, though I seme tame.

♦ ♦ ♦ ♦ ♦

Myne olde dere En'mye, my froward master,
   Afore that Quene, I caused to be acited;
Whiche holdeth the divine parte of nature:
   That, lyke as goolde, in fyre he mought be tryed.
   Charged with dolour, theare I me presented
With horrible feare, as one that greatlye dredith
A wrongfull death, and iustice alwaye seekethe.

And thus I sayde: "Once my lefte foote, Madame,
   When I was yonge I sett within his reigne;
Whearby other then fierlye burninge flame
   I never felt, but many a grevous payne;
   Tourment I suffred, angre, and disdayne,
That myne oppressed patience was past,
And I myne owne life hated at the last.

"Thus hytherto have I my time passed
   In payne and smarte. What wayes proffitable,
How many pleasant dayes have me escaped

In serving this false lyer so deceaveable?
    What witt have wordes so prest and forceable
That may contayne my great myshappynesse,
And iust complayntes of his vngentlenesse?

"O! small honye, muche aloes, and gall!
    In bitternes have my blynde lyfe taisted
His fals swetenes, that torneth as a ball,
    With the amourous dawnce have made me traced;
    And where I had my thought and mynde ataced
From all erthely frailnes and vain pleasure,
He toke me from rest and set me in error.

"He hath made me regarde god muche lesse then I ought,
    And to my self to take right litle heede;
And, for a woman, have I set at nought
    All othre thoughtes, in this onely to spede:
    And he was onely counceillor of this dede,
Alwayes whetting my youthely desyere
On the cruell whetstone tempered with fier.

"But, helas, where nowe had I ever wit,
    Or els any othre gift geven me of nature?
That souner shall chaunge my weryed sprite
    Then the obstinate will, that is my rueler.
    So robbeth my libertie with displeasure
This wicked traytor, whome I thus accuse,
That bitter liff have torned me in pleasaunt vse.

"He hath chased me thorough dyvers regions,
    Thorough desert wodes and sherp high mountaignes,
Thoroughe frowarde people and straite pressions,
    Thorough rocky sees, over hilles and playnes,
    With wery travaill, and labourous paynes;

Alwayes in trouble and in tediousnes,
In all errour and daungerous distres.

"But nother he, nor she, my tother ffoo,
  For all my flyght did ever me forsake;
That though tymely deth hath ben to sloo,
  That, as yet, it hathe me not overtake;
  The hevynly goodenes, of pitie, do it slake:
And note this his cruell extreme tyranny,
That fedeth hym with my care and mysery.

"Syns I was his, owre rested I never,
  Nor loke for to do; and eke the waky nyghtes
The bannysshed slepe may no wyse recouer.
  By deceipte and by force over my sprites
  He is rueler: and syns there neuer bell strikes
Where I ame, that I here not my playntes to renewe,
And he himself, he knoweth that I say is true.

"Ffor never wormes have an old stock eaten,
  As he my hert, where he is alwaye resident;
And doeth the same with deth daily thretyn:
  Thens com the teres and the bitter torment,
  The sighes, the wordes, and eke the languisshement,
That annoye boeth me and peraduenture othre:
Iudge thou that knowest th'one and th'othre."

Myn aduersary, with grevous reprouff,
  Thus he began: "Here, Lady, th'othre part:
That the plain trueth, from which he draweth alowff,
  This vnkynd man shall shew ere that I part.
  In yonge age I toke him from that art
That selleth wordes, and maketh a clattering knyght,
And of my welth I gave him the delight.

"Nowe shameth he not on me for to complain,
   That held him evermore in pleasaunt game
From his desire, that myght have ben his payne;
   Yet onely thereby I broght him to some frame,
   Which as wretchednes he doth greately blame;
And towerd honor I qwickened his wit,
Where els, as a daskard, he myght have sitt.

"He knoweth that Atrides, that made Troye frete,
   And Hannyball to Rome so trobelous,
Whome Homere honoured, Achilles that grete,
   And the Affricane Scipion, the famous,
   And many othre by much vertue glorious,
Whose fame and honor did bryng theim above,
I did let fall, in base dishonest love.

"And vnto him, though he no dele worthy were,
   I chose right the best of many a mylion,
That, vnder the mone, was never her pere
   Of wisdome, womanhode and discretion;
   And of my grace I gave her suche a facon
And eke suche a way, I taught her for to teche
That never base thought his hert myght have reche.

"Evermore, thus, to content his maistres,
   That was his onely frame of honestie.
I sterred him still towerd gentilnes,
   And caused him to regard fidelitie;
   Patiens I taught him in aduersite:
Suche vertues he lerned in my great schole,
Wherof he repenteth, the ignoraunt ffole.

"These were the deceptes and the bitter gall
   That I have vsed, the torment and the anger;

Sweter then for to injoye eny othre in all.
    Of right good seede ill fruyte I gather
    And so hath he that th'unkynde doeth forther.
I norisshe a Serpent vnder my wyng,
And, of his nature, nowe gynneth he to styng.

"And for to tell, at last, my great seruise:
    From thousand dishonestes I have him drawen,
That, by my meanes, in no maner of wyse,
    Never vile pleasure him hath overthrowen;
    Where, in his dede, shame hath him alwaies gnawen,
Dowbting reporte that sholde com to her eare:
Whome now he accuseth he wounted to fere.

"What soever he hath of any honest custume
    Of her and me, that holdeth he every wit;
But lo, there was never nyghtely fantome
    So ferre in errour as he is from his wit
    To plain on vs: he stryveth with the bit,
Which may ruell him and do him pleasure and pain,
And in oon oure make all his greife remayn.

"But oon thing there is above all othre:
    I gave him winges, wherwith he might vpflie
To honor and fame; and, if he would, farther
    Then mortall thinges, above the starry sky;
    Considering the pleasure that an Iye
Myght geve in erthe by reason of his love,
What shuld that be that lasteth still above?

"And he the same himself hath sayed or this,
    But now forgotten is boeth that and I
That gave her him, his onely welth and blisse."
    And at this worde, with dedly shright and cry:

"Thou gave her me," quod I, "but by and by
Thou toke her streight from me, that wo worth thee!"
"Not I," quod he, "but price, that is well worthy."

At last, boeth, eche for himself, concluded;
   I, trembling; but he, with small reverence:
"Lo, thus as we have nowe eche othre accused,
   Dere lady, we wayte onely thy sentence."
   She smyling: "After thissaid audience,
It liketh me," quod she, "to have herd your question,
But lenger tyme doth aske resolution."

◆ ◆ ◆ ◆ ◆

Eche man me telleth I chaunge moost my devise,
   And on my faith me thinck it goode reason
   To chaunge propose like after the season,
Ffor in every cas to kepe still oon gyse
Ys mytt for theim that would be taken wyse;
   And I ame not of suche maner condition,
   But treted after a dyvers fasshion;
   And therupon my dyversnes doeth rise.
But you that blame this dyversnes moost,
   Chaunge you no more, but still after oon rate
   Trete ye me well, and kepe ye in the same state;
And while with me doeth dwell this weried goost,
   My wordes nor I shall not be variable,
   But alwaies oon, your owne boeth ferme and stable.

◆ ◆ ◆ ◆ ◆

Ffarewell Love and all thy lawes for ever:
   Thy bayted hookes shall tangill me no more;
   Senec and Plato call me from thy lore,
   To perfaict welth my wit for to endever.
In blynde error when I did perseuer,
   Thy sherpe repulse that pricketh ay so sore
   Hath taught me to sett in tryfels no store
   And scape fourth, syns libertie is lever.
Therefore farewell: goo trouble yonger hertes
   And in me clayme no more authoritie;
   With idill youth goo vse thy propertie
And theron spend thy many brittil dertes;
   For hetherto though I have lost all my tyme
   Me lusteth no lenger rotten boughes to clymbe.

◆ ◆ ◆ ◆ ◆

My hert I gave the, not to do it payn,
   But to preserue it was to the taken;
   I serued the not to be forsaken,
   But that I should be rewarded again.
I was content thy seruant to remayn,
   But not to be payed vnder this fasshion.
   Nowe syns in the is none othre reason
   Displease the not if that I do refrain.
Vnsaciat of my woo and thy desire,
   Assured be craft to excuse thy fault;
   But syns it please the to fain a default,
Farewell, I say, parting from the fyer:
   For he that beleveth bering in hand
   Plowithe in water and soweth in the sand.

♦ ♦ ♦ ♦ ♦

Ffor to love her for her lokes lovely
My hert was set in thought right fermely,
   Trusting by trouth to have had redresse;
   But she hath made an othre promes
And hath geven me leve full honestly.
Yet do I not reioyse it greatly,
For on my faith I loved to surely;
   But reason will that I do sesse
     For to love her.

Syns that in love the paynes ben dedly,
Me thincke it best that reddely
   I do retorne to my first adresse;
   For at this tyme to great is the prese,
And perilles appere to abundauntely
     For to love her.

♦ ♦ ♦ ♦ ♦

Helpe me to seke for I lost it there,
And if that ye have founde it ye that be here
   And seke to convaye it secretely,
   Handell it soft and trete it tenderly,
Or els it will plain and then appere.
   But rather restore it mannerly,
   Syns that I do aske it thus honestly;
For to lese it, it sitteth me to nere:
     Helpe me to seke.

Alas, and is there no remedy,
But have I thus lost it wilfully?

I wis it was a thing all to dere
    To be bestowed and wist not where.
It was myn hert: I pray you hertely
        Helpe me to seke.

♦ ♦ ♦ ♦ ♦

Som fowles there be that have so perfaict sight,
    Agayn the Sonne their Iyes for to defend,
    And som bicause the light doeth theim offend,
    Do never pere but in the darke or nyght.
Other reioyse that se the fyer bright
    And wene to play in it as they do pretend,
    And fynde the contrary of it that they intend.
    Alas, of that sort I may be by right,
For to withstond her loke I ame not able;
    And yet can I not hide me in no darke place,
    Remembraunce so foloweth me of that face,
So that with tery yen swolne and vnstable,
    My destyne to behold her doeth me lede;
    Yet do I knowe I runne into the glede.

♦ ♦ ♦ ♦ ♦

Bicause I have the still kept fro lyes and blame
    And to my power alwaies have I the honoured,
    Vnkynd tong right ill hast thou me rendred
    For suche deserft to do me wrek and shame.
In nede of succor moost when that I ame
    To aske reward, then standest thou like oon aferd
    Alway moost cold, and if thou speke towerd,
    It is as in dreme vnperfaict and lame.

And ye salt teres again my will eche nyght
   That are with me when fayn I would be alone,
   Then are ye gone when I should make my mone;
And you so reddy sighes to make me shright,
   Then are ye slake when that ye should owtestert;
   And onely my loke declareth my hert.

♦ ♦ ♦ ♦ ♦

Though I my self be bridilled of my mynde,
   Retorning me backeward by force expresse,
   If thou seke honor to kepe thy promes,
   Who may the hold, my hert, but thou thy self vnbynd?
Sigh then no more, syns no way man may fynde
   Thy vertue to let, though that frowerdnes
   Of ffortune me holdeth; and yet, as I may gesse,
   Though othre be present, thou art not all behinde.
Suffice it then that thou be redy there
   At all howres; still vnder the defence
   Of tyme, trouth and love, to save the from offence;
Cryeng *I burne in a lovely desire*
   With my dere maisteres that may not followe,
   Whereby his absence torneth him to sorrowe.

♦ ♦ ♦ ♦ ♦

My galy charged with forgetfulnes
   Thorrough sharpe sees in wynter nyghtes doeth pas
   Twene Rock and Rock; and eke myn ennemy, Alas,
   That is my lorde, sterith with cruelnes;
And every owre a thought in redines,
   As tho that deth were light in suche a case.

An endles wynd doeth tere the sayll apase
Of forced sightes and trusty ferefulnes.
A rayn of teris, a clowde of derk disdain,
    Hath done the wered cordes great hinderaunce;
    Wrethed with errour and eke with ignoraunce.
The starres be hid that led me to this pain;
    Drowned is reason that should me consort,
    And I remain dispering of the port.

♦ ♦ ♦ ♦ ♦

Auysing the bright bemes of these fayer Iyes,
    Where he is that myn oft moisteth and wassheth,
    The werid mynde streght from the hert departeth
    For to rest in his woroldly paradise,
And fynde the swete bitter vnder this gyse.
    What webbes he hath wrought well he perceveth,
    Whereby with himself on love he playneth;
    That spurreth with fyer, and bridilleth with Ise.
Thus is it in suche extremitie brought:
    In frossen thought nowe and nowe it stondeth in flame;
    Twyst misery and welth, twist ernest and game;
But few glad, and many a dyvers thought;
    With sore repentaunce of his hardines:
    Of suche a rote commeth ffruyte fruytles.

♦ ♦ ♦ ♦ ♦

Ever myn happe is slack and slo in commyng
    Desir encresing, myn hope vncertain,
    That leve it or wayt it doeth me like pain,
    And Tigre-like, swift it is in parting.

Alas, the snow shalbe black and scalding;
    The See waterles; fisshe in the mountain;
    The Tamys shall retorne back into his fontain;
    And where he rose the sonne shall take lodging;
Ere that I in this fynde peace or quyetenes,
    Or that love or my lady rightwisely
    Leve to conspire again me wrongfully;
And if that I have after suche bitternes
    Any thing swete, my mouth is owte of tast,
    That all my trust and travaill is but wast.

◆ ◆ ◆ ◆ ◆

Love and fortune and my mynde, remember
    Of that that is nowe, with that that hath ben,
    Do torment me so that I very often
    Envy theim beyonde all mesure.
Love sleith myn hert; fortune is depriver
    Of all my comfort; the folisshe mynde then
    Burneth and plaineth as one that sildam
    Lyveth in rest, still in displeasure.
My plaisaunt dayes they flete away and passe,
    But daily yet the ill doeth chaunge into the wours;
    And more then the half is runne of my cours.
Alas, not of steill but of brickell glasse,
    I see that from myn hand falleth my trust,
    And all my thoughtes are dasshed into dust.

♦ ♦ ♦ ♦ ♦

How oft have I, my dere and cruell foo,
 With those your Iyes for to get peace and truyse,
 Profferd you myn hert, but you do not vse
 Emong so high thinges to cast your mynde so lowe.
Yf any othre loke for it, as ye trowe,
 There vayn weke hope doeth greately them abuse;
 And thus I disdain that that ye refuse;
 It was ons myn: it can no more be so.
Yf I then it chase, nor it in you can fynde
 In this exile no manner of comfort,
 Nor lyve allone, nor where he is called resort,
He may wander from his naturall kynd.
 So shall it be great hurt vnto vs twayn,
 And yours the losse and myn the dedly pain.

♦ ♦ ♦ ♦ ♦

Like to these vnmesurable montayns
 Is my painfull lyff, the burden of Ire,
 For of great height be they, and high is my desire,
 And I of teres, and they be full of fontayns.
Vnder craggy rockes they have full barren playns;
 Herd thoughtes in me my wofull mynde doeth tyre;
 Small fruyt and many leves their toppes do atyre;
 Small effect with great trust in me remayns.
The boystrous wyndes oft their high bowghes do blast
 Hote sighes from me continuelly be shed;
 Cattell in theim, and in me love is fed;
Immoveable ame I, and they are full stedfast;
 Of the restles birdes they have the tune and note,
 And I always plaintes that passe thorough my throte.

* * * * *

Madame, withouten many wordes
    Ons I ame sure ye will or no;
And if ye will, then leve your bordes,
    And vse your wit and shew it so.

And with a beck ye shall me call,
    And if of oon that burneth alwaye
Ye have any pitie at all,
    Aunswer him faire with yea or nay.

Yf it be yea I shalbe fayne;
    If it be nay, frendes as before;
Ye shall an othre man obtain,
    And I myn owne and yours no more.

* * * * *

Ye old mule, that thinck yourself so fayre,
Leve of with craft your beautie to repaire,
    For it is time withoute any fable:
    No man setteth now by riding in your saddell;
To muche travaill so do your train apaire,
      Ye old mule!

With fals favoure though you deceve th'ayes,
Who so tast you shall well perceve your layes
    Savoureth som what of a Kappurs stable,
      Ye old mule!

Ye must now serve to market and to faire,
All for the burden for pannyers a paire;

For syns gray heres ben powdered in your sable,
The thing ye seke for you must yourself enable
To pourchase it by payement and by prayer,
    Ye old mule!

           ◆ ◆ ◆ ◆ ◆

They fle from me that sometyme did me seke
    With naked fote stalking in my chambre.
I have sene theim gentill tame and meke
    That nowe are wyld and do not remembre
    That sometyme they put theimself in daunger
To take bred at my hand; and nowe they raunge
Besely seking with a continuell chaunge.

Thancked be fortune, it hath ben othrewise
    Twenty tymes better; but ons in speciall,
In thyn arraye after a pleasaunt gyse,
    When her lose gowne from her shoulders did fall,
    And she me caught in her armes long and small;
Therewithall swetely did me kysse,
And softely saide, *dere hert, howe like you this?*

It was no dreme: I lay brode waking.
    But all is torned thorough my gentilnes
Into a straunge fasshion of forsaking;
    And I have leve to goo of her goodenes,
    And she also to vse new fangilnes.
But syns that I so kyndely ame serued,
I would fain knowe what she hath deserued.

There was never nothing more me payned,
  Nor nothing more me moved,
As when my swete hert her complayned
  That ever she me loved.
    Alas the while!

With pituous loke she saide and sighed:
  Alas, what aileth me
To love and set my welth so light
  On hym that loveth not me?
    Alas the while!

Was I not well voyde of all pain,
  When that nothing me greved?
And nowe with sorrous I must complain,
  And cannot be releved.
    Alas the while!

My restfull nyghtes and joyfull daies
  Syns I began to love
Be take from me; all thing decayes,
  Yet can I not remove.
    Alas the while!

She wept and wrong her handes withall,
  The teres fell in my nekke;
She torned her face and let it fall;
  Scarsely therewith coulde speke.
    Alas the while!

Her paynes tormented me so sore
  That comfort had I none,

But cursed my fortune more and more
　　To se her sobbe and grone:
　　　　Alas the while!

♦　♦　♦　♦　♦

Ryght true it is, and said full yore agoo:
　　Take hede of him that by thy back the claweth.
For none is wourse then is a frendely ffoo;
　　Though they seme good, all thing that the deliteth,
　　Yet knowe it well, that in thy bosom crepeth:
　　For many a man such fier oft kyndeleth,
　　That with the blase his berd syngeth.

♦　♦　♦　♦　♦

What wourde is that that chaungeth not,
　　Though it be tourned and made in twain?
It is myn aunswer, god it wot,
　　And eke the causer of my payn.
　　A love rewardeth with disdain,
　　Yet is it loved. What would ye more?
　　It is my helth eke and my sore.

♦　♦　♦　♦　♦

Marvaill no more all tho
　　The songes I syng do mone,
For othre liff then wo
　　I never proved none.
And in my hert also

Is graven with lettres diepe
A thousand sighes and mo,
    A flod of teres to wepe.

How may a man in smart
    Fynde matter to rejoyse?
How may a morning hert
    Set fourth a pleasaunt voise?
Play who that can that part:
    Nedes must in me appere
How fortune overthwart
    Doeth cause my morning chere.

Perdy, there is no man
    If he never sawe sight
That perfaictly tell can
    The nature of the light.
Alas, how should I then,
    That never tasted but sowre,
But do as I began,
    Continuelly to lowre?

But yet perchaunce som chaunce
    May chaunce to chaunge my tune;
And when suche chaunce doeth chaunce,
    Then shall I thanck fortune.
And if I have suche chaunce,
    Perchaunce ere it be long
For such a pleasaunt chaunce
    To syng som plaisaunt song.

She sat and sowde that hath done me the wrong,
  Whereof I plain, and have done many a daye;
And whilst she herd my plaint in pitious song,
  Wisshed my hert the samplar as it lay.
The blynd maister whome I have serued so long,
  Grudging to here that he did here her saye,
Made her owne wepon do her fynger blede,
To fele if pricking were so good in dede.

♦ ♦ ♦ ♦ ♦

Tho I cannot your crueltie constrain
For my good will to favor me again,
  Tho my true and faithfull love
  Have no power your hert to move,
    Yet rew vpon my pain.

Tho I your thrall must evermore remain
And for your sake my libertie restrain,
  The greatest grace that I do crave
  Is that ye would vouchesave
    To rew upon my pain.

Tho I have not deserued to obtain
So high Reward but thus to serue in vain,
  Tho I shall have no redresse,
  Yet of right ye can no lesse
    But rew vpon my pain.

But I se well that your high disdain
Wull no wise graunt that I shall more attain;

Yet ye must graunt at the lest
This my powre and small request:
   Rejoyse not at my pain.

◆ ◆ ◆ ◆ ◆

To wisshe and want and not obtain,
To seke and sew esse of my pain,
Syns all that ever I do is vain,
   What may it availl me?

All tho I stryve boeth dey and howre
Against the streme with all my powre,
If fortune list yet for to lowre,
   What may it availl me?

If willingly I suffre woo,
If from the fyre me list not goo,
If then I burne, to plaine me so
   What may it availl me?

And if the harme that I suffre
Be runne to farr owte of mesur,
To seke for helpe any further
   What may it availl me?

What tho eche hert that hereth me plain
Pitieth and plaineth for my payn?
If I no les in greif remain,
   What may it availl me?

Ye, tho the want of my relief
Displease the causer of my greife,

Syns I remain still in myschiefe,
    What may it availl me?

Suche cruell chaunce doeth so me threte
Continuelly inward to fret,
Then of relesse for to trete
    What may it availl me?

Ffortune is deiff vnto my call,
My torment moveth her not at all,
And though she torne as doeth a ball,
    What may it availl me?

Ffor in despere there is no rede;
To want of ere speche is no spede;
To linger still alyve as dede,
    What may it availl me?

◆ ◆ ◆ ◆ ◆

Some tyme I fled the fyre that me brent,
    By see, by land, by water, and by wynd;
And now I folow the coles that be quent
    From Dovor to Calais against my mynde.
Lo! how desire is boeth sprong and spent!
    And he may se that whilome was so blynde;
And all his labor now he laugh to scorne,
Mashed in the breers that erst was all to torne.

◆ ◆ ◆ ◆ ◆

He is not ded that somtyme hath a fall;
   The sonne retorneth that was vnder the clowd;
And when fortune hath spitt oute all her gall,
   I trust good luck to me shalbe allowd.
For I have sene a shippe into haven fall
   After the storme hath broke boeth mast and shrowd;
And eke the willowe that stowpeth with the wynde
Doeth ryse again, and greater wode doeth bynd.

◆ ◆ ◆ ◆ ◆

Th'enmy of liff, decayer of all kynde,
   That with his cold wethers away the grene,
This othre nyght me in my bed did fynde,
   And offered me to rid my fiever clene;
And I did graunt, so did dispaire me blynde.
   He drew his bowe with arrowe sharp and kene,
And strake the place where love had hit before,
And drave the first dart deper more and more.

◆ ◆ ◆ ◆ ◆

Ons as me thought fortune me kyst
   And bad me aske what I thought best;
And I should have it as me list,
   Therewith to set my hert in rest.

I asked nought but my dere hert
   To have for evermore myn owne:

Then at an ende were all my smert,
    Then should I nede no more to mone.

Yet for all that a stormy blast
    Had overtorned this goodely day;
And fortune semed at the last
    That to her promes she saide nay.

But like as oon oute of dispere
    To soudden hope revived I;
Now fortune sheweth herself so fayer
    That I content me wonderly.

My moost desire my hand may reche,
    My will is alwaye at my hand;
Me nede not long for to beseche
    Her that hath power me to commaund

What erthely thing more can I crave?
    What would I wisshe more at my will?
No thing on erth more would I have,
    Save that I have to have it still.

Ffor fortune hath kept her promes
    In graunting me my moost desire:
Of my suffraunce I have redres,
    And I content me with my hiere.

◆ ◆ ◆ ◆ ◆

My lute awake! perfourme the last
Labor that thou and I shall wast,
 And end that I have now begon;
For when this song is sung and past,
 My lute be still, for I have done.

As to be herd where ere is none,
As lede to grave in marbill stone,
 My song may perse her hert as sone;
Should we then sigh, or syng, or mone?
 No, no, my lute, for I have done.

The Rokkes do not so cruelly
Repulse the waves continuelly,
 As she my suyte and affection,
So that I ame past remedy:
 Whereby my lute and I have done.

Prowd of the spoyll that thou hast gott
Of simple hertes thorough loves shot,
 By whome, vnkynd, thou hast theim wone,
Thinck not he haith his bow forgot,
 All tho my lute and I have done.

Vengeaunce shall fall on thy disdain,
That makest but game on ernest pain;
 Thinck not alone vnder the sonne
Vnquyt to cause thy lovers plain,
 All tho my lute and I have done.

Perchaunce the lye wethered and old,
The wynter nyghtes that are so cold,

Playnyng in vain vnto the mone;
Thy wisshes then dare not be told;
  Care then who lyst, for I have done.

And then may chaunce the to repent
The tyme that thou hast lost and spent
  To cause thy lovers sigh and swoune;
Then shalt thou knowe beaultie but lent,
  And wisshe and want as I have done.

Now cesse, my lute, this is the last
Labour that thou and I shall wast,
  And ended is that we begon;
Now is this song boeth sung and past:
  My lute be still, for I have done.

♦ ♦ ♦ ♦ ♦

Nature, that gave the bee so feet a grace
  To fynd hony of so wondrous fashion,
Hath taught the spider owte of the same place
  To fetche poyson, by straynge alteration.
Tho this be straynge, it is a straynger case
  With oon kysse by secret operation
Boeth these at ons in those your lippes to fynde,
In chaunge wherof I leve my hert behinde.

♦ ♦ ♦ ♦ ♦

In eternum I was ons determed
For to have lovid and my minde affermed,

That with my herte it shuld be confermed
    In eternum.

Forthwith I founde the thing that I myght like,
And sought with loue to warme her hert alike,
For, as me thought, I shulde not se the like
    In eternum.

To trase this daunse I put my self in prese;
Vayne hope ded lede and bad I should not cese
To serue, to suffer, and still to hold my pease
    In eternum.

With this furst rule I fordred me apase,
That, as me thought, my trowghthe had taken place
With full assurans to stond in her grace
    In eternum.

It was not long or I by proofe had found
That feble bilding is on feble grounde;
For in her herte this worde ded never sounde,
    In eternum.

In eternum then from my herte I kest
That I had furst determined for the best;
Nowe in the place another thought doeth rest,
    In eternum.

◆ ◆ ◆ ◆ ◆

To cause accord or to aggre,
Two contraries in oon degre,
And in oon poynct, as semeth me,

To all mans wit it cannot be:
    It is impossible.

Of hete and cold when I complain
And say that hete doeth cause my pain,
When cold doeth shake me every vain
And boeth at ons, I say again
    It is impossible.

That man that hath his hert away,
If lyff lyveth there, as men do say,
That he hertles should last on day
Alyve and not to torne to clay,
    It is impossible.

Twixt lyff and deth, say what who sayth,
There lyveth no lyff that draweth breth;
They joyne so nere and eke, i' feith,
To seke for liff by wissh of deth
    It is impossible.

Yet love that all thing doeth subdue,
Whose power ther may no liff eschew,
Hath wrought in me that I may rew
These miracles to be so true,
      That are impossible.

♦ ♦ ♦ ♦ ♦

In dowtfull brest, whilst moderly pitie
    With furyous famyn stondith at debate,
Sayth thebrew moder: "O child vnhappye,
    Retorne thi blowd where thow hadst milk of late.

Yeld me those lymms that I made vnto the,
   And entre there where thou wert generate;
For of on body agaynst all nature
To a nothr must I mak sepulture."

♦ ♦ ♦ ♦ ♦

Off Cartage he, that worthie warier
   Could ouercome but cowld not vse his chaunce;
And I like wise off all my long indeuer,
   The sherpe conquest, tho fortune did avaunce,
Cowld not it vse: the hold that is gyvin ouer
   I vnpossest. So hangith in balaunce
Off warr, my pees, reward of all my payne;
At Mountzon thus I restles rest in Spayne.

♦ ♦ ♦ ♦ ♦

Processe of tyme worketh suche wounder,
   That water which is of kynd so soft
Doeth perse the marbell stone a sonder,
   By litle droppes faling from aloft.

And yet an hert that sems so tender
   Receveth no dropp of the stilling teres,
That alway still cause me to render
   The vain plaint that sowndes not in her eres.

So cruel, alas, is nowght alyve,
   So fiers, so frowerd, so owte of fframe;
But some way, some tyme, may so contryve
   By mens the wild to tempre and tame.

And I that alwaies have sought, and seke
    Eche place, eche tyme for some lucky daye,
This fiers Tigre lesse I fynde her meke
    And more denyd the lenger I pray.

The lyon in his raging furor
    Forberis that sueth mekenes for his boote;
And thou, Alas, in extreme dolor
    The hert so low thou tredis vnder thy foote.

Eche fiers thing lo! how thou doest exceede,
    And hides it vnder so humble a face;
And yet the humble to helpe at nede,
    Nought helpeth tyme, humblenes, nor place.

♦ ♦ ♦ ♦ ♦

From thes hye hilles as when a spryng doth fall,
    It tryllyth downe with still and suttyll corse;
Off this and that it gaders ay, and shall,
    Tyll it have just off flowd the streme and forse,
Then at the fote it ragith ouer all:
    So faryth love when he hath tan a sorse;
His rayne is rage, resistans vaylyth none;
The first estew is remedy alone.

♦ ♦ ♦ ♦ ♦

Tagus, fare well, that westward with thy stremes
    Torns vp the grayns off gold alredy tryd:
With spurr and sayle for I go seke the Tems
    Gaynward the sonne that shewth her welthi pryd

And to the town which Brutus sowght by drems
   Like bendyd mone doth lend her lusty syd.
My Kyng, my Contry alone for whome I lyve,
Of myghty love the winges for this me gyve.

♦ ♦ ♦ ♦ ♦

Off purpos Love chase first for to be blynd,
   For he with sight of that that I behold
Vanquisht had bene against all godly kynd;
   His bow your hand and trusse shold have vnfold,
And he with me to serve had bene assind:
   But, for he blind and rekelesse wolde him hold,
And still by chaunse his dedly strokes bestow,
With such as see I serve and suffer wow.

♦ ♦ ♦ ♦ ♦

Ys yt possyble
That so hye debate,
So sharpe, so sore, and off suche rate,
Shuld end so sone and was begone so late?
Is it possyble?

Ys yt possyble
So cruell intent,
So hasty hete and so sone spent,
Ffrom love to hate, and thens ffor to Relent?
Is it possyble?

Ys yt possyble
That eny may fynde

Within on hert so dyverse mynd,
To change or torne as wether and wynd?
  Is it possyble?

  Is it possyble
   To spye yt in an Iye
  That tornys as oft as chance on dy?
The trothe whereoff can eny try?
  Is it possyble?

  It is possyble
   Ffor to torne so oft,
  To bryng that lowyste that wasse most aloft,
And to fall hyest yet to lyght sofft:
  It is possyble.

  All ys possyble
   Who so lyst beleve;
  Trust therfore fyrst, and after preve;
As men wedd ladyes by lycence and leve,
  All ys possyble.

♦ ♦ ♦ ♦ ♦

As power and wytt wyll me Assyst,
My wyll shall wyll evyn as ye lyst.

Ffor as ye lyst, my wyll ys bent
In euery thyng to be content,
To serve in love tyll lyff be spent,
And to Reward my love thus ment,
  Evyn as ye lyst.

To fayn or fable ys not my mynd,
Nor to Refuce suche as I fynd,
But as a lambe of humble kynd,
Or byrd in cage, to be Assynd
        Evyn as ye lyst.

When all the flokk ys cum and gone,
Myn eye and hart agreythe in one,
Hathe chosyn yow only Alone
To be my joy, or elles my mone,
        Evyn as ye lyst.

Joy, yf pytty apere in place,
Mone, yf dysdayn do shew hys face;
Yet crave I not as in thys case
But as ye lede, to follow the trace
        Evyn as ye lyst.

Sum in wordes muche love can fayn,
And sum for wordes gyve wordes agayn;
Thus wordes for wordes in wordes Remayn,
And yet at last wordes do optayn
        Evyn as ye lyst.

To crave in wordes I wyll exchew,
And love in dede I wyll ensew;
Yt ys my mynd bothe hole and trew,
And for my trewthe I pray yow rew
        Evyn as ye lyst.

Dere hart, I bydd your hart farewell
With better hart than tong can tell;
Yet take thys tale as trew as gospell;

Ye may my lyff save or expell
    Evyn as ye lyst.

◆ ◆ ◆ ◆ ◆

The knott whych ffyrst my hart dyd strayn,
    Whan that your servant I becam,
Doth bynde me styll for to Remayne
    All waies your owne, as nowe I am:
And yff ye fynde that I do ffayn,
    With just judgement my selffe I dam
      To haue dysdayn.

Iff other thowght in me do growe
    Butt styll to love yow stedefastly,
Yff that the profe do nott well showe
    That I am yowrs assueredly,
Lett euery welth turne me to woo,
    And yow to be contynually
      My chefest foo.

Yff other love or newe request
    Do ese my hart, but only thys,
Or yf within my weryd brest
    Be hyd one thowght that mene amys,
I do desyer that myne vnrest
    May styll encrease, and I to myss
      That I love best.

Yff in my love ther be one spott
    Off false deceyte or doblenes,
Or yff I mynde to slypp thys knott

By want of fayth or stedefastnes,
Lett all my sarwyes be forgott,
    And when I would have cheefe redresse
      Esteme me nott.

But yff that I consume in payn
    Of burnynge syghes and fervent love,
And daly seke non other gayn
    But with my dede thes wordes to prove,
Me thynke off Ryght I shuld optayne
    That ye wulde mynde for to remove
      Yowr gret dysdayn.

And for the ende off thys my songe
    Vnto yowr handys I do submytt
My dedly greff and payns so stronge,
    Whych in my harte be fermly shytt:
And when ye lyst, redresse my wronge,
    Syns well ye knowe this paynfull fytt
      Hath last to longe.

◆ ◆ ◆ ◆ ◆

It was my choyse, yt was no chaunce
    That browght my hart in others holde,
Wherby ytt hath had sufferaunce
    Lenger, perde, then Reason wold;
Syns I ytt bownd where ytt was free
    Me thynkes ywys of Ryght yt shold
      Acceptyd be.

Acceptyd be withowte Refuse,
    Vnles that fortune have the power

All Ryght of love for to abuse;
    For, as they say, one happy howre
May more prevayle then Ryght or myght,
    Yf fortune then lyst for to lowre,
        What vaylyth Right?

What vaylyth Ryght yff thys be trew?
    Then trust to chaunce and go by gesse
Then who so lovyth may well go sew,
    Vncerten hope for hys redresse.
Yett some wolde say assueredly
    Thou mayst appele for thy relesse
        To fantasy.

To fantasy pertaynys to chose:
    All thys I knowe, for fantasy
Ffurst vnto love dyd me induse;
    But yet I knowe as stedefastly
That yff love haue no faster knott,
    So nyce a choyse slyppes sodenly.
        Yt lastyth nott.

Itt lastyth not that stondes by change;
    Fansy doth change; fortune ys frayle:
Both thes to plese the way ys strange.
    Therfore me thynkes best to prevayle:
Ther ys no way that ys so just
    As trowgh to lede, tho tother fayle,
        And therto trust.

♦ ♦ ♦ ♦ ♦

Syns loue ys suche that, as ye wott,
   Cannot always be wysely vsyd,
I say therfore then blame me nott,
   Tho I therin haue ben abusyd;
   Ffor as with cause I am accusyd,
Gyllty I graunt, suche was my lott,
   And tho yt cannot be excusyd
Yet let suche folye be forgott.

Ffor in my yeres of rekles youthe
   Me thought the power of loue so gret
That to her lawes I bound my trouthe
   And to my wyll there was no lett.
   Me lyst nomore so far to fett
Suche frute lo as of loue ensewthe;
   The gayn was small that was to gett,
And of the losse the lesse the reuthe.

And few there ys but fyrst or last
   A tyme in loue ons shall they haue;
And glad I am my tyme ys past,
   Henceforthe my fredome to withsaue.
   Now in my hart there shall I grave
The groundyd grace that now I tast;
   Thankyd be fortune that me gave
So fayre a gyfft, so sure and fast.

Now suche as haue me sene or thys,
   When youthe in me sett forthe hys kynd,
And foly framd my thought amys,
   The faute wherof now well I ffynd,
   Loo, syns that so yt ys assynd

That vnto eche a tyme there ys,
   Then blame the lott that led my mynd
Sometyme to lyue in loves blys.

But frome henceforthe I do protest
   By presse of that that I haue past,
Shall neuer ceace within my brest
   The power of loue so late owt cast;
   The knott therof ys knytt ffull fast,
And I therto so sure proffest,
   Ffor euermore with me to last
The power wherin I am possest.

♦ ♦ ♦ ♦ ♦

My loue ys lyke vnto th'eternall fyre,
   And I as those whyche therin do remayn,
Whose grevous paynes ys but theyre gret desyre
   To se the syght whyche they may not attayn.
So in helles heate my self I fele to be,
That am restraynd by gret extremyte
The syght of her whyche ys so dere to me.
   O puissant loue and power of gret avayle,
   By whome hell may be fellt or dethe assayle!

♦ ♦ ♦ ♦ ♦

Fforget not yet the tryde entent
Of suche a truthe as I haue ment,
My gret travayle so gladly spent
    Fforget not yet.

Fforget not yet when fyrst began
The wery lyffe ye know syns whan,
The sute, the seruys none tell can.
    Fforgett not yett.

Fforget not yet the gret assays,
The cruell wrong, the skornfull ways,
The paynfull pacyence in denays,
    Fforgett not yet.

Fforget not yet, forget not thys,
How long ago hathe ben and ys
The mynd that neuer ment amys,
    Fforget not yet.

Fforget not then thyn owne aprovyd,
The whyche so long hathe the so lovyd,
Whose stedfast faythe yet neuer movyd,
    Fforget not thys.

◆ ◆ ◆ ◆ ◆

O myserable sorow withowten cure
  Yf it plese the, lo, to haue me thus suffir,
At lest yet let her know what I endure,
  And this my last voyse cary thou thether
  Wher lyved my hope now ded for ever;
For as ill grevus is my banyshement
As was my plesur whan she was present.

◆ ◆ ◆ ◆ ◆

Blame not my lute for he must sownde
   Of thes or that as liketh me;
For lake of wytt the lutte is bownde
   To gyve suche tunes as plesithe me:
Tho my songes be sume what strange,
And spekes suche wordes as toche thy change,
     Blame not my lutte.

My lutte, alas, doth not ofende,
   Tho that perforus he must agre
To sownde suche teunes as I entende
   To sing to them that hereth me;
Then tho my songes be some what plain,
And tochethe some that vse to fayn,
     Blame not my lutte.

My lute and strynges may not deny,
   But as I strike they must obay;
Brake not them than soo wrongfully,
   But wryeke thy selff some wyser way:
And tho the songes whiche I endight
Do qwytt thy chainge with rightfull spight,
     Blame not my lute.

Spyght askyth spight and changing change,
   And falsyd faith must nedes be knowne;
The faute so grett, the case so strainge,
   Of right it must abrode be blown:
Then sins that by thyn own desartt
My soinges do tell how trew thou artt,
     Blame not my lute.

Blame but the selffe that hast mysdown
   And well desaruid to haue blame;
Change thou thy way, so evyll bygown,
   And then my lute shall sownde that same:
But if tyll then my fyngeres play
By thy desartt their wontyd way,
      Blame not my lutte.

Farwell, vnknowne, for tho thow brake
   My strynges in spight with grett desdayn,
Yet haue I fownde owtt for thy sake
   Stringes for to strynge my lute agayne;
And yf perchance this folysh Rymyme
Do make the blushe at any tyme,
      Blame nott my lutte.

◆ ◆ ◆ ◆ ◆

Perdye I saide yt not
   Nor never thought to do,
As well as I ye wott
   I have no powre thereto;
And if I ded, the lott
   That first ded me enchaine
Do never slake the knott
   But strayt it to my payne.

And if I ded, eche thing
   That maye do harme or woo
Contynuallye maye wring
   My herte whereso I goo;
Reporte maye always ring
   Of shame of me for aye,

Yf yn my herte ded spring
   The worde that ye doo saye.

Yf I saide so, eche sterre
   That is yn heven above
Maye frowne on me to marre
   The hope I have yn love;
And if I ded, suche warre
   As they brought vnto Troye
Bring all my lyf afarre
   From all this luste and joye.

And if I ded so saye,
   The bewtye that me bounde
Encresse from daye to daye
   More cruell to my wounde,
With all the mone that maye
   To playnte maye torne my song;
My lif maye sone dekaye
   Without redresse bye wrong.

Yf I be clere fro thought,
   Whye do ye then complaine?
Then ys this thing but sought
   To torne me to more payne.
Then that that ye haue wrought
   Ye must yt now redresse;
Of right therefore ye ought
   Suche Rigor to represse.

And as I haue deseruid,
   So graunte me nowe my hire;
Ye kno I never swervid,
   Ye never fownd me lyre.

For Rachell have I seruid,
   (For Lya carid I never)
And her I have Reseruid
   Within my herte for ever.

◆ ◆ ◆ ◆ ◆

Sins you will nedes that I shall sing,
   Take yt in worth siche as I have,
Plentye of plaint, mone and morning,
   Yn depe dispaire and dedlye payne,
Boteles for boote, crying to crave,
     To crave yn vayne.

Suche hammers worke within my hed
   That sounde nought els vnto my eris
But faste at borde and wake abed:
   Suche tune the tempre to my song
To waile my wrong, that I wante teris
     To waile my wrong.

Dethe and dispaire afore my face,
   My dayes dekaes, my grefe doth gro;
The cause thereof is in this place,
   Whom crueltye dothe still constraine
For to reioise, tho yt be wo
     To here me plaine.

A brokin lute, vntunid stringes
   With such a song maye well bere parte,
That nether pleasith him that singes
   Nor theim that here, but her alone

That with her herte wold straine my herte
　　To here yt grone.

Yf it greve you to here this same
　That you do fele but in my voyse,
Considre then what plesaunt game
　I do sustaine in everye parte
To cause me sing or to reioyse
　　Within my herte.

♦ ♦ ♦ ♦ ♦

　Me list no more to sing
　Of love nor of suche thing,
　Howe sore that yt me wring;
　　For what I song or spake
　　Men dede my songis mistake.

　My songes ware to defuse,
　Theye made folke to muse;
　Therefor, me to excuse,
　　Theye shall be song more plaine,
　　Nothr of joye nor payne.

　What vaileth then to skippe
　At fructe over the lippe?
　　For frute withouten taste
　　Dothe noght but rott and waste.

　What vailith vndre kaye
　To kepe treasure alwaye,
　That never shall se daye?

Yf yt be not vsid,
Yt ys but abusid.

What vayleth the flowre
To stond still and whither?
Yf no man yt savour,
    Yt servis onlye for sight
    And fadith towardes night.

Therefore fere not t'assaye
To gadre ye that maye
The flower that this daye
    Is fresher than the next:
    Marke well, I saye, this text.

Let not the frute be lost
That is desired moste;
Delight shall quite the coste.
    Yf hit be tane in tyme,
    Small labour is to clyme.

And as for siche treasure
That makithe the the richer,
And no dele the porer,
    When it is gyven or lente
    Me thinkes yt ware well spente.

Yf this be undre miste,
And not well playnlye wyste,
Vndrestonde me who lyste;
    For I reke not a bene,
    I wott what I doo meane.

◆ ◆ ◆ ◆ ◆

To Rayle or geste ye kno I vse yt not,
  Though that such cause some tyme in folkes I finde:
  And tho to chaung ye list to sett your minde,
  Love yt who liste, in faithe I like yt not.
And if ye ware to me as ye are not,
  I wolde be lothe to se you so unkinde;
  But sins your faithe muste nedes be so, be kinde:
  Tho I hate yt, I praye you leve yt not.
Thinges of grete waight I neuer thought to crave:
  This is but small—of right denye yt not.
  Your fayning wayis as yet forget them not,
But like rewarde let other lovers have:
  That is to saye, for seruis true and faste,
  To long delaies and changing at the laste.

◆ ◆ ◆ ◆ ◆

What shulde I saye
  Sins faithe is dede,
And truthe awaye
  From you ys fled?
  Shulde I be led
With doblenesse?
Naye, naye, mistresse!

I promiside you
  And you promisid me
To be as true
  As I wolde bee;
  But sins I se

Your doble herte,
Farewell my perte!

Though for to take
    Yt ys not my minde
But to forsake—
    I am not blind—
    And as I finde
So will I truste.
Farewell, vniuste!

Can ye saye naye?
    But you saide
That I allwaye
    Shulde be obeide;
    And thus betraide
Or that I wiste—
Fare well, vnkiste!

♦ ♦ ♦ ♦ ♦

Dyvers dothe vse as I have hard and kno,
    When that to chaunge ther ladies do beginne,
    To morne and waile, and neuer for to lynne,
    Hoping therbye to pease ther painefull woo.
And some ther be, that when it chanseth soo
    That women change and hate where love hath bene,
    Thei call them fals, and think with woordes to wynne
    The hartes of them wich otherwhere dothe gro.
But as for me, though that by chaunce indede
    Change hath outworne the favor that I had,
    I will not wayle, lament, nor yet be sad;
Nor call her fals that falsley ded me fede:

But let it passe and think it is of kinde,
That often chaunge doth plese a womans minde.

◆ ◆ ◆ ◆ ◆

The losse is small to lese such one,
That shrynckith for a slendr naye;
And wyt thei lak that wolde mak mone,
Tho all such peakes ware wipid awaye.

◆ ◆ ◆ ◆ ◆

Spight hathe no powre to make me sadde
Nor scornefulnesse to make me playne;
Yt doth suffise that ons I had,
And so to leve yt is no payne.

Let theim frowne on that leste dothe gaine,
Who ded reioise must nedes be gladd;
And tho with wordis thou wenist to rayne,
Yt doth suffise that ons I had.

Sins that in chekes thus overthwarte
And coylye look is thou doste delight,
Yt doth suffise that myne thou warte,
Tho change hathe put thye faithe to flight.

Alas, it is a pevishe spight
To yelde thiself and then to parte,
But sins thou setst thie faithe so light,
Yt doth suffise that myne thou warte.

And sins thye love dothe thus declyne
   And in thye herte suche hate dothe grow,
Yt dothe suffise that thou warte myne,
   And with good will I quite yt soo.

   Some tyme my frende, fare well my foo,
Sins thou change I am not thyne,
   But for relef of all my woo
Yt dothe suffise that thou warte myne.

Prayeng you all that heris this song
   To iudge no wight, nor none to blame;
Yt dothe suffise she dothe me wrong
   And that herself doth kno the same.

   And tho she chaing, it is no shame;
Theire kinde it is and hathe bene long;
   Yet I proteste she hath no name:
Yt dothe suffise she dothe me wrong.

◆ ◆ ◆ ◆ ◆

Grudge on who liste, this ys my lott,
No thing to want if it ware not.

My yeris be yong even as ye see,
All thinges thereto doth well agre,
Yn faithe, in face, in eche degre
No thing doth wante, as semith me,
   If yt ware not.

Some men dothe saye that frendes be skarce,
But I have founde as in this cace

A frende wiche gyvith to no man place,
But makis me happiest that euer was,
    Yf it were not.

Grudge on who list, this is my lot,
No thing to want if yt ware not.

A hart I have besidis all this,
That hathe my herte and I have his;
If he dothe well yt is my blis,
And when we mete no lak there is
    Yf it ware not.

Yf he can finde that can me please,
A thinckes he dois his owne hertes ease;
And likewise I coulde well apease
The chefest cause of his misease,
    Yf it ware not.

Grudge on who list, this is my lot,
No thing to want if it ware not.

A master eke god hath me sente,
To hom my will is hollye bente,
To serue and love for the intente
That bothe we might be well contente,
    Yf it ware not.

And here an ende: yt dothe suffise
To speke fewe wordes among the wise.
Yet take this note before your eyes:
My mirthe shulde doble ons or twise,
    Yf it ware not.

Grudge on who list, this is my lot,
No thing to want if it ware not.

♦ ♦ ♦ ♦ ♦

Hate whome ye list, for I kare not;
Love whom ye list and spare not;
Do what ye list and drede not;
Think what ye liste, I fere not:
For as for me I am not,
But even as one that reckes not
Whyther ye hate or hate not;
For yn your love I dote not;
Wherefore I praye you, forget not,
But love whom ye liste, ffor I care not.

♦ ♦ ♦ ♦ ♦

Greting to you bothe yn hertye wyse
   As vnknowen I sende, and this mye entente
As I do here, you to aduertyse,
   Lest that perchaunce your deades you do repente.
   The vnknowen man dredes not to be shente,
But sayes as he thinkes: so fares yt bye me,
That nother ffere nor hope in no degree.

The bodye and the sowle to holde togiddre,
   Yt is but right and reason woll the same,
And ffryndelie the oon to love the other
   Yt incresith your brute and also your fame;
   But marke well my wordes, for I fere no blame:

Truste well your selves, but ware ye trust no mo,
For suche as ye think your frende maye fortune be your ffo.

Beware hardelye ere ye have enye nede,
    And to frendes reconsilide trust not greatelye;
Ffor theye that ons with hastie spede
    Exiled them selves out of your companye,
    Though theye tourne againe and speke farelye,
Fayning them selves to be your frendes faste,
Beware of them, for theye will disseyeve you at laste.

Fayre wordes makis ffoolys fayne,
    And bering in hande causith moche woo,
For tyme tryeth trothe, therefore refrayne:
    And from suche as be redye to doo—
    None doo I name but this I kno,
That bye this faute cause causith moche,
Therefore beware if yo do know anye suche.

To wise folkes fewe wordes is an old sayeng;
    Therefore at this tyme I will write nomore,
But this short lesson take fore a warninge:
    Bye soche light frendes sett littill store;
    Yf ye do othere wise ye will repent yt sore.
And thus of this lettre making an ende,
To the boddye and the sowle I me commend.

Wryting lyfles at the manner place
    Of him that hathe no chave nore no were dothe dwell,
But wandering in the wilde worlde, wanting that he hase,
    And nother hopis nor ffearis heven nor hell;
    But lyvith at adventure, ye kno him full well,

The twentie daye of marche he wrote yt yn his house,
And hathe him recommendyd to the kat and the mowse.

♦ ♦ ♦ ♦ ♦

Wyth seruing still
    This have I wone,
For my godwill
    To be vndone;

And for redresse
    Of all my payne,
Disdaynefulnes
    I have againe.

And for reward
    Of all my smarte
Lo, thus vnharde,
    I must departe!

Wherefore all ye
    That after shall
Bye ffortune be,
    As I am, thrall,

Example take
    What I have won,
Thus for her sake
    To be vndone!

◆ ◆ ◆ ◆ ◆

Dryven bye desire I dede this dede,
    To daunger my self without cause whye,
To truste the vntrue, not like to spede,
    To speke and promise faithefullie;
    But now the proof dothe verifie
That who so trustithe or he kno
Dothe hurte himself and please his ffoo.

◆ ◆ ◆ ◆ ◆

I abide and abide and better abide,
    And after the olde prouerbe, the happie daye;
    And ever my ladye to me dothe saye:
    "Let me alone and I will prouyde."
I abide and abide and tarrye the tyde,
    And with abiding spede well ye maye:
    Thus do I abide I wott allwaye,
    Nother obtayning nor yet denied.
Aye me! this long abidyng
    Semithe to me as who sayethe
    A prolonging of a dieng dethe
Or a refusing of a desyred thing.
    Moche ware it bettere for to be playne
    Then to saye "abide" and yet shall not obtayne.

◆ ◆ ◆ ◆ ◆

Patiens, for I have wrong,
    And dare not shew whereyn,
Patiens shalbe my song,

Sins truthe can no thing wynne;
    Patiens then for this fytt,
    Hereafter commis not yett.

♦ ♦ ♦ ♦ ♦

Luckes, my faire falcon, and your fellowes all,
    How well plesaunt yt were your libertie!
Ye not forsake me that faire might ye befall.
    But they that somtyme lykt my companye,
Like lyse awaye from ded bodies thei crall:
    Loe, what a profe in light adversytie!
But ye, my birdes, I swear by all your belles,
Ye be my fryndes, and so be but few elles.

♦ ♦ ♦ ♦ ♦

A face that shuld content me wonders well
    Shuld not be faire but louelie to behold,
With gladsome cheare all grief for to expell;
    With sober lookes so wold I that it should
Speake without wordes, such woordes as non can tell;
    The tresse also should be of crysped gold;
With witt: and thus might chaunce I might be tyde,
And knyt agayne the knott that should not slide.

♦ ♦ ♦ ♦ ♦

Like as the byrde in the cage enclosed,
    The dore vnsparred and the hawke without,
Twixte deth and prison piteously oppressed,

Whether for to chose standith in dowt:
  Certes! so do I, wyche do syeke to bring about
Wyche shuld be best by determination—
By losse off liefe libertye, or liefe by preson.

Oh! myscheffe by myscheffe to be redressed!
  Wher payne is the best ther lieth litell pleasure:
By schort deth out off daunger yet to be delyuered,
  Rather then with paynfull lieffe, thraldome and doloure;
  Ffor small plesure moche payne to suffer;
Soner therfore to chuse, me thincketh it wysdome,
By losse off life lybertye then liefe by preson.

By leynght off liefe yet shulde I suffer,
  Adwayting time and fortunes chaunce:
Manye thinges happen within an hower;
  That wyche me oppressed may be avaunce.
  In time is trust, wyche by deathes greuaunce
Is vtterlye lost: then were it not reson
By deathe to chuse libertye, and not lieffe by preson?

But deathe were deliueraunce and liefe lengthe off payne;
  Off two ylles, let see nowe, chuse the best:
This birde to deliuer, youe that here her playne,
  Your aduise, yowe louers! wyche shalbe best?
  In cage in thraldome, or by the hauke to be opprest?
And which for to chuse, make playne conclusyon:
By losse off liefe libertye, or liefe by prison?

◆ ◆ ◆ ◆ ◆

The piller pearisht is whearto I lent,
  The strongest staye of myne vnquyet mynde;
  The lyke of it no man agayne can fynde,
  Ffrom East to West, still seking thoughe he went.
To myne vnhappe! for happe away hath rent
  Of all my ioye the vearye bark and rynde;
  And I (alas) by chaunce am thus assynde
  Dearlye to moorne till death do it relent.
But syns that thus it is by destenye,
  What can I more but have a wofull hart,
  My penne in playnt, my voyce in carefull crye,
My mynde in woe, my bodye full of smart,
  And I my self, my self always to hate,
  Till dreadfull death do ease my dolefull state?

◆ ◆ ◆ ◆ ◆

A Ladye gave me a gyfte she had not;
And I receyvid her guifte I toke not:
She gave it me willinglye and yet she wold not;
And I receyvid it, albeit I coulde not.
If she geve it me, I force not;
And yf she take it agayne, she cares not:
Conster what this is, and tell not,
Ffor I am fast sworne—I maye not.

♦ ♦ ♦ ♦ ♦

Stond who so list vpon the Slipper toppe
   Of courtes estates, and lett me heare reioyce;
And vse me quyet without lett or stoppe,
   Vnknowen in courte, that hath suche brackishe ioyes:
      In hidden place, so lett my dayes forthe passe,
That when my yeares be done, withouten noyse,
   I may dye aged after the common trace.
For hym death greep'the right hard by the croppe
      That is moche knowen of other; and of him self alas,
   Doth dye vnknowen, dazed with dreadfull face.

♦ ♦ ♦ ♦ ♦

Passe forth, my wonted cryes,
   Those cruell eares to pearce,
Which in most hatefull wyse
   Doe styll my plaintes reuerse.
Doe you, my teares, also
   So wet her barrein hart,
That pitye there may grow
   And crueltie depart.

For though hard rockes among
   She semes to haue bene bred,
And of the Tigre long
   Bene nourished and fed:
Yet shall that nature change,
   If pitie once win place,
Whom as vnknowen and strange
   She now away doth chase.

And as the water soft,
    Without forcyng or strength,
Where that it falleth oft,
    Hard stones doth perse at length:
So in her stony hart
    My plaintes at last shall graue,
And, rygour set apart,
    Winne grant of that I craue.

Wherfore, my plaintes, present
    Styll so to her my sute,
As ye, through her assent,
    May bring to me some frute;
And as she shall me proue,
    So bid her me regarde,
And render loue for loue:
    Which is a iust reward.

◆ ◆ ◆ ◆ ◆

Mystrustfull mindes be moued
    To haue me in suspect:
The troth it shalbe proued,
    Which time shall once detect.

Though falshed go about
    Of crime me to accuse,
At length I do not doute
    But truth shall me excuse.

Such sawce as they haue serued
    To me without desart,

Euen as they haue deserued,
    Therof god send them part.

♦ ♦ ♦ ♦ ♦

For shamefast harm of great and hatefull nede,
In depe despayre, as did a wretch go
With ready corde out of his life to spede.
His stumbling foote did finde an hoorde, lo!
Of golde, I say, where he preparde this dede:
And, in eschange, he left the corde tho.
    He that had hidde the golde and founde it not,
    Of that he founde he shapte his neck a knot.

♦ ♦ ♦ ♦ ♦

In court to serue decked with freshe aray,
Of sugred meates felyng the swete repast,
The life in bankets, and sundry kindes of play
Amid the presse of lordly lokes to waste
Hath with it ioynde oft times such bitter taste,
    That who so ioyes such kinde of life to holde,
    In prison ioyes, fettred with cheines of gold.

♦ ♦ ♦ ♦ ♦

If thou wilt mighty be, flee from the rage
    Of cruell wyll, and see thou kepe thee free
From the foule yoke of sensuall bondage;
    For though thy empyre stretche to Indian sea,

And for thy feare trembleth the fardest Thylee,
If thy desire haue ouer thee the power,
Subiect then art thou and no gouernour.

If to be noble and high thy minde be meued,
   Consider well thy grounde and thy beginnyng;
For he that hath eche starre in heauen fixed,
   And geues the Moone her hornes and her eclipsyng,
   Alike hath made the noble in his workyng,
So that wretched no way thou may bee,
Except foule lust and vice do conquere thee.

All were it so thou had a flood of golde
   Vnto thy thirst, yet should it not suffice;
And though with Indian stones, a thousande folde
   More precious then can thy selfe deuise,
   Ycharged were thy backe, thy couitise
And busye bytyng yet should neuer let
Thy wretchid life ne do thy death profet.

SATIRES

◆ ◆ ◆ ◆ ◆

Myne owne John Poynz, sins ye delight to know
   The cause why that homeward I me drawe,
   And fle the presse of courtes wher soo they goo,
Rather then to lyve thrall, vnder the awe
   Of lordly lokes, wrappid within my cloke,
   To will and lust lerning to set a lawe;
It is not for becawse I skorne or moke
   The powar of them, to whome fortune hath lent
   Charge over vs, of Right, to strike the stroke:

But true it is that I have allwais ment
    Lesse to estime them then the common sort,
    Of owtward thinges that juge in their intent,
Withowt regarde what dothe inwarde resort.
    I grawnt sumtime that of glorye the fyar
    Dothe touche my hart: me lyst not to report
Blame by honowr and honour to desyar.
    But how may I this honour now atayne
    That cannot dy the coloure blak a lyer?
My Poynz, I cannot frame me tune to fayne,
    To cloke the trothe for praisse withowt desart,
    Of them that lyst all vice for to retayne.
I cannot honour them that settes their part
    With Venus and Baccus all theire lyf long;
    Nor holld my pece of them allthoo I smart.
I cannot crowche nor knelle to do so grete a wrong,
    To worship them, lyke gode on erthe alone,
    That ar as wollffes thes sely lambes among.
I cannot with my wordes complayne and mone,
    And suffer nought; nor smart wythout complaynt,
    Nor torne the worde that from my mouthe is gone.
I cannot speke and loke lyke a saynct,
    Vse wiles for witt and make deceyt a pleasure,
    And call crafft counsell, for proffet styll to paint.
I cannot wrest the law to fill the coffer
    With innocent blode to fede my sellff fat,
    And doo most hurt where most hellp I offer.
I am not he that can alow the state
    Off highe Caesar and dam Cato to dye,
    That with his dethe dyd skape owt off the gate
From Caesares handes (if Lyve do not lye)
    And wolld not lyve whar lyberty was lost:
    So did his hert the commonn wele aplye.
I am not he suche eloquence to boste,

To make the crow singing as the swane,
Nor call the lyon of cowarde bestes the moste
That cannot take a mows as the cat can:
And he that dithe for hungar of the golld
Call him Alessaundre; and say that Pan
Passithe Apollo in musike manyfolld;
Praysse Syr Thopas for a nobyll talle,
And skorne the story that the knyght tolld.
Praise him for counceill that is droncke of ale;
Grynne when he laugheth that bereth all the swaye,
Frowne when he frowneth and grone when he is pale;
On othres lust to hang boeth nyght and daye:
None of these poyntes would ever frame in me;
My wit is nought—I cannot lerne the waye.
And much the lesse of thinges that greater be,
That asken helpe of colours of devise
To joyne the mene with eche extremitie,
With the neryst vertue to cloke alwaye the vise:
And as to pourpose like wise it shall fall,
To presse the vertue that it may not rise;
As dronkenes good felloweshippe to call;
The frendly ffoo with his dowble face
Say he is gentill and courtois therewithall;
And say that Favell hath a goodly grace
In eloquence; and crueltie to name
Zele of justice and chaunge in tyme and place;
And he that sufferth offence withoute blame
Call him pitefull; and him true and playn
That raileth rekles to every mans shame.
Say he is rude that cannot lye and fayn;
The letcher a lover; and tirannye
To be the right of a prynces reigne.
I cannot, I. No, no, it will not be.
This is the cause that I could never yet

Hang on their slevis that way as thou maist se
A chippe of chaunce more then a pownde of witt.
  This maketh me at home to hounte and to hawke
  And in fowle weder at my booke to sitt.
In frost and snowe then with my bow to stawke,
  No man doeth marke where so I ride or goo;
  In lusty lees at libertie I walke,
And of these newes I fele nor wele nor woo,
  Sauf that a clogg doeth hang yet at my hele:
  No force for that for it is ordered so,
That I may lepe boeth hedge and dike full well.
  I ame not now in Ffraunce to judge the wyne,
  With saffry sauce the delicates to fele;
Nor yet in Spaigne where oon must him inclyne
  Rather then to be, owtewerdly to seme.
  I meddill not with wittes that be so fyne,
Nor Fflaunders chiere letteth not my sight to deme
  Of black and white, nor taketh my wit awaye
  With bestlynes, they beeste do so esteme;
Nor I ame not where Christe is geven in pray
  For mony, poison and traison at Rome,
  A commune practise vsed nyght and daie:
But here I ame in Kent and Christendome
  Emong the muses where I rede and ryme;
  Where if thou list, my Poynz, for to come,
Thou shalt be judge how I do spend my tyme.

♦ ♦ ♦ ♦ ♦

My mothers maydes when they did sowe and spynne,
  They sang sometyme a song of the feld mowse,
  That forbicause her lyvelood was but thynne,
Would nedes goo seke her townysshe systers howse.

She thought her self endured to much pain,
  The stormy blastes her cave so sore did sowse,
That when the forowse swymmed with the rain
  She must lye cold and whete in sorry plight;
  And wours then that, bare meet there did remain
To comfort her when she her howse had dight,
  Sometyme a barly corne, sometyme a bene,
  For which she laboured hard boeth daye and nyght,
In harvest tyme whilest she myght goo and glyne;
  And when her stoore was stroyed with the flodd,
  Then wellawaye! for she vndone was clene.
Then was she fayne to take in stede of fode
  Slepe if she myght her hounger to begile.
  "My syster" (quoth she) "hath a lyving good,
And hens from me she dwelleth not a myle.
  In cold and storme she lieth warme and dry
  In bed of downe; the dyrt doeth not defile
Her tender fote. She laboureth not as I.
  Richely she fedeth and at the richemans cost,
  And for her meet she nydes not crave nor cry.
By se, by land, of delicates the moost
  Her Cater sekes and spareth for no perell;
  She fedeth on boyled, bacon meet, and roost,
And hath therof neither charge nor travaill;
  And when she list the licor of the grape
  Doeth glad her hert, till that her belly swell."
And at this jorney she maketh but a jape;
  So fourth she goeth trusting of all this welth
  With her syster her part so for to shape
That if she myght kepe her self in helth
  To lyve a Lady while her liff doeth last.
  And to the dore now is she come by stelth,
And with her foote anon she scrapeth full fast.
  Th'othre for fere durst not well scarse appere,

Of every noyse so was the wretche agast.
At last she asked softly who was there,
   And in her langage as well as she cowd,
   "Pepe," quoth the othre syster, "I ame here."
"Peace," quoth the towny mowse, "Why spekest thou so lowde?"
   And by the hand she toke her fayer and well.
   "Welcome," quoth she, "my sister by the Roode!"
She fested her, that joy it was to tell
   The faere they had: they drancke the wyne so clere.
   And as to pourpose now and then it fell
She chered her with "How, syster, what chiere?"
   Amyddes this joye befell a sorry chaunce
   That well aweye! the straunger bought full dere
The fare she had; for as she loked ascaunce,
   Vnder a stole she spied two stemyng Ise
   In a rownde hed with sherp erys. In Fraunce
Was never mowse so ferd for tho the vnwise
   Had not Isene suche a beest before,
   Yet had nature taught her after her gyse
To knowe her ffoo and dred him evermore.
   The towney mowse fled: she knewe whether to goo.
   Th'othre had no shift but wonders sore,
Fferd of her liff: at home she wyshed her tho,
   And to the dore, alas, as she did skippe—
   Thevyn it would, lo, and eke her chaunce was so—
At the threshold her sely fote did trippe,
   And ere she myght recover it again
   The traytor Catt had caught her by the hippe
And made her there against her will remain,
   That had forgotten her poure suretie and rest
   For semyng welth wherin she thought to rayne.
Alas, my Poynz, how men do seke the best,
   And fynde the wourst by error as they stray!
   And no marvaill: when sight is so opprest,

And blynde the gyde, anon owte of the way
  Goeth gyde and all in seking quyete liff.
  O wretched myndes, there is no gold that may
Graunt that ye seke! No warr, no peace, no stryff,
  No, no, all tho thy hed were howpt with gold,
  Sergeaunt with mace, hawbert, sword nor knyff
Cannot repulse the care that folowe should.
  Eche kynd of lyff hath with hym his disease.
  Lyve in delight evyn as thy lust would,
And thou shalt fynde when lust doeth moost the please
  It irketh straite and by it self doth fade.
  A small thing it is that may thy mynde apese.
Non of ye all there is that is so madde
  To seke grapes vpon brambles or breers,
  Nor none, I trow, that hath his wit so badd
To set his hay for Conys over Ryvers,
  Ne ye set not a dragg net for an hare,
  And yet the thing that moost is your desire
Ye do mysseke with more travaill and care.
  Make playn thyn hert that it be not knotted
  With hope or dred, and se thy will be bare
Ffrom all affectes whome vice hath ever spotted;
  Thy self content with that is the assigned,
  And vse it well that is to the allotted.
Then seke no more owte of thy self to fynde
  The thing that thou haist sought so long before,
  For thou shalt fele it sitting in thy mynde.
Madde, if ye list to continue your sore,
  Let present passe and gape on tyme to come
  And diepe your self in travaill more and more.
Hens fourth, my Poynz, this shalbe all and some:
  These wretched fooles shall have nought els of me
  But to the great god and to his high dome
None othre pain pray I for theim to be

But when the rage doeth led them from the right
That lowking backwards vertue they may se
Evyn as she is so goodly fayre and bright;
And whilst they claspe their lustes in armes a crosse,
Graunt theim, goode lorde, as thou maist of thy myght,
To frete inwards for losing suche a losse.

♦ ♦ ♦ ♦ ♦

A spending hand that alway powreth owte
Had nede to have a bringer in as fast,
And on the stone that still doeth tourne abowte
There groweth no mosse: these proverbes yet do last.
Reason hath set theim in so sure a place
That length of yeres their force can never wast.
When I remember this and eke the case
Where in thou stondes, I thowght forthwith to write,
Brian, to the, who knowes how great a grace
In writing is to cownsell man the right.
To the, therefore, that trottes still vp and downe,
And never restes, but runnyng day and nyght
Ffrom Reaulme to Reaulme, from cite, strete and towne.
Why doest thou were thy body to the bones,
And myghtst at home slepe in thy bed of downe
And drynck goode ale so noppy for the noyns,
Fede thy self fat and hepe vp pownd by pownd?
Lykist thou not this? *No.* Why? *For swyne so groyns*
In stye and chaw the tordes molded on the grownd,
And dryvell on perilles, the hed still in the maunger,
Then of the harp the Asse to here the sownd.
So sackes of durt be filled vp in the cloyster
That servis for lesse then do thes fatted swyne.
Tho I seme lene and dry withoute moyster,

Yet woll I serve my prynce, my lord and thyn,
And let theim lyve to fede the panche that list,
So I may fede to lyve both me and myn.
By god, well sayde! But what and if thou wist
How to bryng in as fast as thou doest spend?
That would I lerne, And it shall not be myst
To tell the how. Now hark what I intend.
Thou knowst well first who so can seke to plese
Shall pourchase frendes where trowght shall but offend.
Ffle therefore trueth: it is boeth welth and ese.
For tho that trouth of every man hath prayse,
Full nere that wynd goeth trouth in great misese.
Vse vertu as it goeth now a dayes:
In word alone to make thy language swete,
And of the dede yet do not as thou sayse;
Elles be thou sure thou shalt be farr vnmyt
To get thy bred, eche thing is now so skant.
Seke still thy proffet vpon thy bare fete.
Lend in no wise, for fere that thou do want,
Onles it be as to a dogge a chese;
By which retorne be sure to wyn a kant
Of half at lest: it is not goode to lese.
Lerne at Kittson that in a long white cote
From vnder the stall withoute landes or feise
Hath lept into the shopp; who knoweth by rote
This rule that I have told the here before.
Sumtyme also riche age begynneth to dote:
Se thou when there thy gain may be the more.
Stay him by the arme, where so he walke or goo;
Be nere alway: and if he koggh to sore,
When he hath spit tred owte and please him so.
A diligent knave that pikes his maisters purse
May please him so that he withouten mo
Executor is: and what is he the wourse?

But if so chaunce you get nought of the man,
   The wedow may for all thy charge deburse.
A ryveld skyn, a stynking breth, what than?
   A tothles mowth shall do thy lips no harme:
   The gold is good and tho she curse or ban,
Yet where the list thou maist ly good and warme;
   Let the old mule byte vpon the bridill,
   Whilst there do ly a swetter in thyn arme.
In this also se you be not Idell:
   Thy nece, thy cosyn, thy sister or thy doghter,
   If she be faire, if handsom be her myddell,
Yf thy better hath her love besoght her,
   Avaunce his cause and he shall help thy nede.
   It is but love: turne it to a lawghter.
But ware, I say, so gold the helpe and spede.
   That in this case thow be not so vnwise
   As Pandare was in suche a like dede;
Ffor he, the ffooll, of conscience was so nyse
   That he no gayn would have for all his payne.
   Be next thy self, for frendshipp beres no prise.
Laughst thou at me? Why, do I speke in vayne?
   No, not at the, but at thy thrifty gest.
   Wouldest thou I should for any losse or gayne
Chaunge that for gold that I have tan for best
   Next godly thinges, to have an honest name?
   Should I leve that, then take me for a best!
Nay then, farewell! And if thou care for shame,
   Content the then with honest pouertie,
   With fre tong what the myslikes to blame,
And for thy trouth sumtyme aduersitie:
   And therewithall this thing I shall the gyve—
   In this worould now litle prosperite,
And coyne to kepe as water in a syve.

PSALMS

Psalm 37. Noli emulari

Altho thow se th'owtragius clime aloft,
   Envie not thowe his blinde prosperitye;
   The welth of wretches, tho it semith soft,
Move not thy hert by theyre felicity.
   They shalbe found like grasse turnd into hay,
   And as the herbes that wither sodenlye.
Stablisshe thy trust in god, seke right allway,
   And on the yerth thowe shalte inhabite longe;
   Ffede and encreace such hope from day to day,
And if with god thow time thy hartie songe
   He shal the giue what soo thy hart can lust.
   Cast vppon god thy will that right thy wrong;
Gyve him the charge, for he vpright and iust
   Hath cure of the and of thy cares all,
   And he shall make thy trowgh to be discust
Bright as the sone, and thy rightwisnes shall
   (The cursids welth tho now do it deface)
   Shine like the daylight that we the none call.
Paciently abide the Lordes assured grace;
   Bere with even minde the trouble that he sendes;
   Dismay the not tho thou se the purchace
Encresse of some, for such like lucke god sendes
   To wicked folke [—so prosper the untrue.]
   Restrayne thy mind from wrath that ay offendes;
Do way all rage, and see thou do eschewe
   By theire like dede suche dedes for to committ:
   Ffor wikked folke their overthrow shal rewe.
Who pacientlie abid and do not flitt,
   They shall possede the world from heire to hayre:

The wikked shall of all his welth be quitt
So sodainly and that without repaire
    That all his pomp and his staring aray
    Shall from thyn Iye departe as blast of ayre.
The sobre thenne the world shall weld, I say,
    And live in welth and pes soo plentifull.
    Him to distroy the wikked shall assay
And gnasshe his teethe eke with girninge yrefull.
    The Lorde shall scorne the threatninges of the wretche,
    Ffor he doth know the tyde is nighe at full
When he shall syncke and no hand shall hym seeche.
    They have vnsheathed eke their blouddye bronds
    And bent theire bowe to prove if they might reache
To overthrowe the [just; stretched forth their honds,]
    Bare of relief the harmelesse to devoure.
    The sworde shall pearce the hart of suche that fonds;
Theire bow shall breake in their moste endevoure.
    A little livinge gotten rightfullie
    Passithe the ritchesse and eke the highe powre
Of that that wretches have gatherd wickedlye.
    Pearishe shall the wickedes posteritie,
    And god shall stablishe the iuste assuredlye.
The iust mans dayes the Lorde doth know and see,
    Their heritage shall laste for evermore,
    And of their hope beguylde they shall not be.
When dismolde dayes shall wrappe the t'other sore,
    They shall be full when other faynte for foode;
    Thearwhyl'ste shall faile theise wicked men thearfore.
To godes ennemyes suche end shall be allowdd
    As hath Lambs greace wastinge in the fyre,
    That is consumde into a smokye clowde.
Borow'th th'vniust without will or desyre
    To yelde agayne; the iuste freelye dothe geve,

Wheare he seethe neede as marcye dothe requyre
Who will'the hym well for right thearfore shall leve;
    Who bannyshe hym shall be rooted awaye;
    His steppes shall god directe still and relieve,
And please hym shall what lyf hym lust assaye;
    And thoughe he fall vnder foote lye shall not he;
    Catchinge his hand for god shall streight hym staye.
[The righteous yet, though age has stolen on me,
    Forsaken by the Lord I ne'er have seen,]
    Nor yet his seede foodelesse seeme for to be.
The iuste to all men mercyfull hathe bene,
    Busye to do well: thearfore his seede, I saye,
    Shall have habundaunce all waye fresshe and grene.
Fflee yll, do good, that thow may'ste last allwaye,
    Ffor god dothe love for evermore th'vpright:
    Never his Chosen dothe he cast awaye;
Ffor ever he them myndeth daye and night,
    And wicked seede alwaye shall waste to nought:
    The iuste shall welde the worlde as their owne rights
And longe thearon shall dwell as theye have wrought.
    Withe wisdome shall the wyse mans mowthe hym able;
    His tongue shall speake alwaye even as it ought;
With godes learninge he hathe his harte stable;
    His foote thearfore from slydinge shall be sure.
    The wicked watchethe the iust for to disable,
And for to se hym dothe his busye cure;
    But god will not suffer hym for to quaile
    By tyrannye, nor yet bye faulte vnpure
To be condemn'd in iudgement without faile.
    Awayte thearfore the commynge of the Lorde;
    Live withe his Lawes in pacience to prevayle,
And he shall raise the of thyne owne accorde
    Above the earth, in suretye to beholde
    The wickedes deathe, that thow maye it recorde.

I have well seene the wycked sheene lyke goolde,
   Lustie and grene as Lawrell lasting aye;
   But even anon and scantt his seate was colde:
When I have paste agayne the self same waye,
   Wheare he did raigne, he was not to be fownde;
   Vanyshte he was for all his fresshe arraye.
Let vprightnes be still thie stedfast grownde.
   Ffollowe the right: suche one shall alwaye fynde
   Hym self in peace and plentie to habounde.
All wicked folke reversyd shall vntwynde,
   And wretchidnes shall be the wickedes ende:
   Healthe to the iuste from god shall be assignde.
He shall them strengthe, whome troble shoulde offend:
   The Lord shall helpp, I saye, and them delyver
   Ffrom curssed handes, and healthe vnto them send,
For that in Hym they sett their truste for ever.

Th'Argument

Somtyme the pryde of mye assured trothe
   Contemned all helpp of god and eke of man:
But when I saw man blyndlye how he goi'the
   In demyng hartes, whiche none but god there can,
And his domes hyd, wheareby mans Malyce grow'th;
   Myne Earle, this doute my hart did humble than,
Ffor errour so might murder Innocence.
Then sang I thus in god my Confydence.

♦ ♦ ♦ ♦ ♦

Love to gyve law vnto his subiect hertes
   Stode in the Iyes of Barsabe the bryght;
And in a look annone hymsellff convertes,
   Cruelly plesant byfore kyng David syght;
First dasd his Iyes, and forder forth he stertes,
   With venemd breth as sofftly as he myght
Towcht his sensis and ouerronnis his bonis
With creping fyre, sparplid for the nonis.

And when he saw that kendlid was the flame,
   The moyst poyson in his hert he launcyd,
So that the sowle did tremble with the same;
   And in this brawle as he stode and trauncyd,
Yelding vnto the figure and the frame
   That those fayre Iyes had in his presens glauncid,
The forme that love had printyd in his brest
He honorth it as thing off thinges best.

So that forgott the wisdome and fore-cast
   (Wych wo to Remes when that thes kynges doth lakk)
Forgettyng eke goddes maiestie as fast
   Ye, and his own, forthwith he doth to mak
Vrye to go into the feld in hast,
   Vrye, I say, that was his Idolles mak,
Vnder pretence off certen victorye,
For enmy's swordes a redy pray to dye.

Wherby he may enjoy her owt of dowt,
   Whom more then god or hymsellff he myndyth;
And after he had browght this thing abowt
   And off that lust posest hym sellff, he fyndyth
That hath and doth reuerse and clene torn owt

Kynges from kyndomes and cytes vndermyndyth:
He blyndyd thinkes this trayne so blynd and closse
To blynd all thing that nowght may it disclosse.

But Nathan hath spyd owt this trecherye
    With rufull chere, and settes afore his face
The gret offence, outrage and Iniurye,
    That he hath done to god as in this Case,
By murder for to clok Adulterye;
    He shewth hym ek from hevyn the thretes, alas;
So sternly sore this prophet, this Nathan,
That all amasid this agid woofull man:

Lyke hym that metes with horrour and with fere,
    The hete doth strayt forsake the lymms cold,
The colour eke drowpith down from his chere,
    So doth he fele his fyer maynifold.
His hete, his lust and plesur all in fere
    Consume and wast; and strayt his crown of gold,
His purpirll pall, his sceptre he lettes fall,
And to the ground he throwth hymsellff withall.

The pompous pryd of state and dygnite
    Forthwith rabates repentant humblenes;
Thynner vyle cloth then clothyth pouerte
    Doth skantly hyde and clad his nakednes;
His faire, hore berd of reverent gravite
    With ruffeld here knowyng his wykednes:
More lyke was he the sellff same repentance
Then statly prynce off worldly governance.

His harpe he taketh in hand to be his guyde,
    Wherwith he offerth his plaintes his sowle to save,
That from his hert distilles on euery syde,

Withdrawyng hym into a dark Cave
Within the grownd wherin he myght hym hyde,
   Fleing the lyght, as in pryson or grave:
In wych as sone as David enterd had,
The dark horrour did mak his fawte a drad.

But he withowt prolonging or delay
   Rof that that myght his lord, his god, apese,
Fallth on his knees and with his harp, I say,
   Afore his brest, frawtyd with disese
Off stormy syghes, his chere coulourd lyk clay,
   Dressyd vpryght, seking to conterpese
His song with syghes, and towching of the strynges
With tendre hert, Lo thus to god he synges.

Psalm 6. Domine ne in furore

O Lord, sins in my mowght thy myghty name
   Sufferth it sellff my Lord to name and call,
   Here hath my hert hope taken by the same;
That the repentance wych I have and shall
   May at thi hand seke marcy as the thing,
   Only confort of wrechid synners all;
Wherby I dare with humble bymonyng
   By thy goodnes off the this thing require:
   Chastyse me not for my deserving,
Acordyng to thy just conceyvid Ire.
   O Lord, I dred; and that I did not dred
   I me repent, and euermore desyre
The, the to dred. I open here and spred
   My fawte to the; but thou, for thi goodnes,
   Mesure it not in Largenes nor in bred.
Punish it not, as askyth the grettnes

Off thi furour, provokt by my offence.
Tempre, O Lord, the harme of my excesse
With mendyng will, that I for recompense
Prepare agayne; and rather pite me,
For I ame wek and clene withowt defence:
More is the nede I have of remede,
For off the hole the Leche takyth no cure.
The shepe that strayth the sheperd sekes to se:
I, lord, ame stray'd; I, sek withowt recure,
Fele al my lymms, that have rebelld for fere,
Shake in dispayre onles thou me assure.
Mye flesshe is troubled, my hart doth feare the speare;
That dread of death, of death that ever lastes,
Threateth of right and draweth neare and neare.
Moche more my sowle is trowbled by the blastes
Of theise assawltes that come as thick as hayle
Of worldlye vanytie, that temptacion castes
Agaynst the weyke bulwarke of the flesshe frayle:
Wheare in the sowle in great perplexitie
Ffeelethe the sensis, with them that assayle,
Conspyre, corrupte by vse and vanytie;
Whearby the wretche dothe to the shade resorte
Of hope in the, in this extreamytie.
But thow, O Lord, how longe after this sorte
Fforbearest thow to see my myserye?
Suffer me yet, in hope of some comforte,
Ffeare and not feele that thow forgettest me.
Returne, O Lorde, O Lorde, I the beseche,
Vnto thie olde wonted benignitie.
Reduce, revyve my sowle: be thow the Leche,
And reconcyle the great hatred and stryfe
That it hath tane agaynste the flesshe, the wretche
That stirred hathe thie wrathe bye filthie life.
Se how mye sowle doth freat it to the bones,

Inwarde remorce so sharp'the it like a knife;
That but thow helpp the caitife, that bemones
His great offence, it turnes anon to dust.
Heare hath thie mercye matter for the nones;
Ffor if thie rightwise hand that is so iuste
Suffer no Synne or stryke with dampnacion,
Thie infinyte marcye want nedes it must
Subjecte matter for his operacion:
For that in deth there is no memorie
Amonge the Dampnyd, nor yet no mencion
Of thie great name, grownd of all glorye.
Then if I dye and goe wheare as I feare
To thinck thearon, how shall thie great mercye
Sownde in my mowth vnto the worldes eare?
Ffor theare is none that can thee lawde and love,
Ffor that thow nilt no love among them theare.
Suffer my Cryes thie marcye for to move,
That wonted is a hundred yeares offence
In momente of repentaunce to remove.
How ofte have I calde vpp with diligence
This slowthful flesshe longe afore the daye
Ffor to confesse his faulte and negligence;
That to the done for ought that I coold say
Hath still returnd to shrowde it self from colde;
Whearbye it suffers nowe for suche delaye.
By nightlye playntes in stede of pleasures olde
I wasshe my bed with teares contynuall,
To dull my sight that it be never bolde
To stirr mye hart agayne to suche a fall.
Thus drye I vpp among my foes in woe,
That with my fall do rise and grow with all,
And me bysett evin now, where I am so,
With secrett trapps to troble my penaunce.
Sum do present to my weping yes, lo,

The chere, the manere, bealte and countenaunce
  Off her whose loke, alas, did mak me blynd.
  Sum other offer to my remembrans
Those plesant wordes now bitter to my mynd;
  And sum shew me the powre of my armor,
  Tryumph and conquest, and to my hed assind
Dowble diademe. Sum shew the favor
  Of peple frayle, palais, pompe, and ryches,
  To thes marmaydes and theyre baytes off error.
I stopp myn eris with help of thy goodnes;
  And for I fele it comith alone of the
  That to my hert thes foes have non acces,
I dare them bid: *Avoyd wreches and fle!*
  The lord hath hard the voyce off my complaint;
  Your engins take no more effect in me.
The lord hath herd, I say, and sen me faynt
  Vnder your hand and pitith my distres.
  He shall do mak my sensis by constraint
Obbey the rule that reson shall expres,
  Wher the deceyte of yowr glosing baite
  Made them vsurpe a powre in all exces.
Shamid be thei all that so ly in whaite
  To compas me, by missing of theire pray!
  Shame and rebuke redound to suche decayte!
Sodayne confusion's strok withowt delay
  Shall so defface theire craffty sugestion
  That they to hurt my helthe no more assay,
Sins I, O lord, remayne in thi protection.

Who so hathe sene the sikk in his fevour,
  Affter treux taken with the hete or cold
And that the fitt is past off his faruour,
  Draw faynting syghes, let hym, I say, behold
Sorowfull David affter his langour,
  That with the terys that from his iyes down rold,
Pausid his plaint and layd adown his harp,
Faythfull record of all his sorows sharp.

It semid now that of his fawt the horrour
  Did mak aferd no more his hope of grace,
The thretes whereoff in horrible errour
  Did hold his hert as in dispaire a space,
Till he had willd to seke for his socour
  Hym selff accusing, beknowyng his cace,
Thinking so best his Lord for to apese,
Eesd, not yet heled, he felith his disese.

Semyth horrible no more the dark Cave
  That erst did make his fault for to tremble,
A place devout or refuge for to save;
  The socourles it rather doth resemble:
For who had sene so knele within the grave
  The chieff pastor of thebrews assemble
Wold juge it made by terys of penitence
A sacrid place worthi off reuerence.

With vapord iyes he lokyth here and there,
  And when he hath a while hymsellff bethowght,
Gadryng his sprites that were dismayd for fere;
  His harp agayne into his hand he rowght,
Tunyng accord by jugement of his ere:

His hertes botum for a sigh he sowght,
And there withall apon the holow tre
With straynid voyce agayne thus cryth he.

♦ ♦ ♦ ♦ ♦

Lik as the pilgryme that in a long way
　　Fayntyng for hete, provokyd by some wind
In some fresh shaade lith downe at mydes off day,
　　So doth off David the weryd voyce and mynd
Tak breth off syghes when he had song this lay,
　　Vnder such shaad as sorow hath assynd;
And as the tone still myndes his viage end,
So doth the tother to mercy still pretend.

On sonour cordes his fingers he extendes,
　　Withowt heryng or jugement off the sownd;
Down from his iyes a streme off terys discendes
　　Withowt feling that trykill on the grownd,
As he that bledes in baigne ryght so intendes
　　Th'altryd sensis to that that they ar bownd;
But syght and wepe he can non othr thing,
And lok vp still vnto the hevins kyng.

But who had bene withowt the Cavis mowth,
　　And herd the terys and syghes that he did strayne,
He wold have sworne there had owt off the sowth
　　A lewk warme wynd browght forth a smoky rayne;
But that so close the Cave was and vnkowth
　　That none but god was record off his payne:
Elles had the wynd blowne in all Israells erys
The woffull plaint and off theire kyng the terys.

Off wych some part, when he vpp suppyd hade,
   Lik as he whom his owne thowght affrays,
He torns his look. Hym semith that the shade
   Off his offence agayne his force assays
By violence dispaire on hym to lade:
   Stertyng like hym whom sodeyne fere dismays,
His voyce he strains, and from his hert owt brynges
This song that I not wyther he crys or singes.

Psalm 51. Miserere mei, Domine

Rew on me, lord, for thy goodnes and grace,
   That off thy nature art so bountefull,
   Ffor that goodnes that in the world doth brace
Repugnant natures in quiete wonderfull;
   And for thi mercys nomber withowt end
   In hevin and yerth perceyvid so plentefull
That ouer all they do them sellffes extend:
   Ffor those marcys much more then man can synn
   Do way my synns that so thy grace offend.
Agayne washe me, but washe me well within,
   And from my synn that thus makth me affrayd
   Make thou me clene, as ay thy wont hath byn.
Ffor vnto the no nombre can be layd
   For to prescrybe remissions off offence
   In hertes retornd, as thow thy sellff hast sayd.
And I beknow my ffawt, my neclegence,
   And in my syght my synn is fixid fast,
   Theroff to have more perfett penitence.
To the alone, to the have I trespast,
   Ffor none can mesure my fawte but thou alone;
   For in thy syght I have not bene agast
For to offend, juging thi syght as none,

So that my fawt were hid from syght of man,
  Thy maiestye so from my mynd was gone:
This know I and repent. Pardon thow than,
  Wherby thow shalt kepe still thi word stable,
  Thy justice pure and clene; by cawse that whan
I pardond ame, then forthwith justly able,
  Just I ame jugd by justice off thy grace.
  Ffor I my sellff, lo thing most vnstable,
Fformd in offence, conceyvid in like case,
  Ame nowght but synn from my natyvite.
  Be not this sayd for my excuse, alase,
But off thy help to shew necessite:
  Ffor lo thou loves the trowgh off inward hert,
  Wich yet doth lyve in my fydelite;
Tho I have fallen by fraylte ouerthwart,
  Ffor willfull malice led me not the way,
  So much as hath the fleshe drawne me apart.
Wherfore, O lord, as thow hast done alway,
  Tech me the hydden wisdome off thy lore,
  Sins that my fayth doth not yet dekay;
And as the juyz do hele the liepre sore
  With hysope clense, clense me, and I ame clene.
  Thow shalt me washe, and more then snow therfore
I shall be whight. How fowle my fawt hath bene!
  Thow off my helth shalt gladsome tydynges bryng,
  When from above remission shall be sene
Descend on yerth: then shall for joye vpspryng
  The bonis that were afore consumed to dust.
  Looke not, O lord, apon myn offendyng,
But do away my dedes that ar vnjust.
  Make a clene hert in the myddes off my brest
  With spryte vpryght, voydyd from fylthye lust.
Ffrom thyn iys cure cast me not in vnrest,
  Nor take from me thy spryte of holynesse.

Rendre to me joye off thy help and rest;
My will conferme with spryte off stedfastnesse:
    And by this shall thes goodly thinges ensue.
    Sinners I shall in to thy ways adresse:
They shall retorne to the and thy grace sue.
    My tong shall prayse thy justification
    My mowgh shall spred thy gloryus praysis true.
But off thi sellff, O god, this operation
    It must proced by purging me from blood,
    Among the just that I may have relation;
And off thy lawdes for to let owt the flood,
    Thow must, O lord, my lypps furst vnlose:
    Ffor if thou hadst estemid plesant good
The owtward dedes that owtward men disclose,
    I wold have offerd vnto the sacryfice.
    But thou delyghtes not in no such glose
Off owtward dede, as men dreme and devyse.
    The sacryfice that the lord lykyth most
    Is spryte contrite. Low hert in humble wyse
Thow dost accept, O god, for plesant host.
    Make Syon, Lord, accordyng to thy will,
    Inward Syon, the Syon of the ghost:
Off hertes Hierusalem strengh the walles still.
    Then shalt thou take for good thes vttward dedes,
    As sacryfice thy plesure to fullfyll.
Off the alone thus all our good procedes.

♦ ♦ ♦ ♦ ♦

    I se the change ffrom that that was,
        And how thy ffayth hath tayn hes fflyght;
    But I with pacyence let yt pase
        And with my pene thys do I wryt

To show the playn be prowff off syght:
    I se the change.

I se the change off weryd mynd,
    And sleper hold hath quet my hyer;
Lo! how by prowff in the I ffynd
    A bowrnyng ffath in changyng ffyer.
    Ffarwell my part, prowff ys no lyer!
    I se the change.

I se the change off chance in loue;
    Delyt no lenger may abyd.
What shold I sek ffurther to proue?
    No, no, my trust, ffor I haue tryd
    The followyng of a ffallse gyd:
    I se the change.

I se the change as in thys case
    Has mayd me ffre ffrom myn avoo;
Ffor now another has my plase,
    And or I wist, I wot ner how,
    Yt haf net thys as ye here now:
    I se the change.

I se the change, seche ys my chance
    To sarue in dowt and hope in weyn;
But sens my surty so doth glance,
    Repentans now shall quyt thy payn,
    Neuer to trust the lyke agayne:
    I se the change.

About the Editor

❖❖

W. S. Merwin was born in New York and has lived in France, Spain, Portugal, England, Mexico, and Hawaii, as well as his native city. He is the author of twelve books of poems, most recently The Rain in the Trees *(Alfred A. Knopf, 1988) and* Selected Poems *(Atheneum, 1988), in addition to three volumes of prose and seventeen of translation; and he has received, among many awards, the Pulitzer Prize, the Bollingen Award, the Fellowship of the Academy of American Poets, and the PEN Translation Prize. He lives in Hawaii with his wife, Paula.*